THE SECRET
LANGUAGE OF SYMBOLS

THE SECRET LANGUAGE OF SYMBOLS

A VISUAL KEY TO SYMBOLS
AND THEIR MEANINGS

BY DAVID FONTANA

CHRONICLE BOOKS
SAN FRANCISCO

The Secret Language of Symbols
David Fontana

First published in the United States in 1994 by Chronicle Books

Cover photograph: Victoria and Albert Museum, London/E.T. Archive

Conceived, Edited and Designed by
Duncan Baird Publishers
Highlight House
57 Margaret Street
London W1N 7FG

Editor: Marek Walisiewicz
Designer: Jeniffer Harte
Commissioned artwork: Hannah Firmin/Sharp Practice
Picture research: Julia Brown

Library of Congress Cataloging-in-Publication Data

Fontana, David.
    The secret language of symbols: a visual key to symbols and their meanings /
David Fontana.
            p.   cm.
    Includes index.
    ISBN 0-8118-0462-3   ISBN 0-8118-0489-5
    1. Symbolism (Psychology) 2. Symbolism--History. I. Title.
BF458.F56 1994
302.2'22--dc20   93-10297
                                                                         CIP

Typeset in Sabon
Color reproduction by Colourscan, Singapore
Printed by Imago, Singapore

Distributed in Canada by
Raincoast Books
112 East Third Avenue
Vancouver, B.C. V5T 1C8

10 9 8 7 6 5 4 3 2 1

Chronicle Books
275 Fifth Street
San Francisco, CA 94103

"Truth did not come into the world naked, but it came in types and images. One will not receive the truth in any other way...The bridegroom must enter through the image into the truth."

The Gospel of Saint Philip

Contents

Introduction

Symbols are profound expressions of human nature. They have occurred in all cultures at all times, and from their first appearance in Paleolithic cave paintings they have accompanied the development of civilization. However, symbols are more than just cultural artefacts: in their correct context, they still speak powerfully to us, simultaneously addressing our intellect, emotions and spirit. Their study is the study of humanity itself.

Human communication depends largely on signs in the form of written or spoken words, images or gestures. These signs are merely representations of reality – consciously made and readily recognizable echoes of objects, actions and concepts in the world around us. They are intended to be precise in their significance: maps, roadsigns, the words in a textbook and the sounds we make to give instructions are all designed to convey information succinctly and unambiguously. But there is another aspect of symbolism that is equally important though less explicit – the side that relates to our inner psychological and spiritual world. Within this inner world, a symbol can represent some deep intuitive wisdom that eludes direct expression.

Older civilizations recognized the power of symbols and used them extensively in their art, religions, myths and rituals. Although they are often dismissed by Western rationalism, the inner significance of symbols is undiminished today, and they still appear frequently in art, literature and film, and in the stories loved by successive generations of children. Deep-rooted symbols are used subliminally and cynically in advertisements, and even in the images and rhetoric of political campaigns. For most people, the most profound symbols are confronted most frequently in dreaming; they are also seen in the spontaneous paintings and drawings produced by children and by patients in psychotherapy.

Dr Carl Gustav Jung, the Swiss psychologist and psychotherapist, to whom we owe much of our knowledge of the importance of symbols in our psychological life, distinguished symbols from the consciously invented signs of everyday life, defining them as "terms, names, or even pictures that may be familiar in daily life, yet that possess specific connotations in addition to their conventional and obvious meanings. They imply something vague, hidden, and unknown to us." A symbol generates itself from the unconscious as a spontaneous expression of some deep

inner power of which we are aware, but cannot fully encapsulate in words. As such, the symbol becomes, in Jung's words, "a perpetual challenge to our thoughts and feelings. That probably explains why a symbolic work is so stimulating, why it grips us so intensely ...". Certain kinds of symbolism constitute a universal language, because the images and their meanings occur in similar forms – and carry similar power – right across cultures and centuries. The symbols that go to make up this language are the natural expression of inner psychological forces.

Perhaps because of an intuitive awareness of the part they play in our inner lives, and because of the way in which they resonate with our emotions, people tend to be drawn to symbols and readily develop an interest in them. The aim of the present book is to respond to and stimulate this interest and, drawing upon psychology, Eastern and Western spirituality, anthropology and history, to provide easy access into the symbolic world.

Hieroglyphics
The earliest form of Egyptian script – hieroglyphic – is an intriguing mixture of signs and symbols. Its characters are stylized but recognizable pictures of natural or man-made objects, some of which convey meaning, while others have phonetic value. Although it appears primitive, hieroglyphic is capable of holding the same level of meaning as our own language. The script was considered sacred, and was used mainly in religious and ceremonial contexts.

Emblems
Symbols may become assimilated into signs or emblems, whose purpose is mainly to provide a badge for identification. In this 15th-century painting, the Christian symbol of the three fishes (see page 88) appears as an heraldic emblem.

The Jungian View

Modern theories about the meanings and uses of symbols are derived largely from the pioneering work of Carl Gustav Jung. In analysing the dreams of diverse patients – normal, neurotic and psychotic – Jung noted the recurrence of certain deeply symbolic images, such as the "apparently universal symbol ... (of) the mandala" (see page 60). He was also struck by the similarity between the images that emerged during analysis and the symbols appearing in Eastern and Western religions, myths, legends and rituals, particularly those of esoteric movements, such as alchemy (see page 146). Jung concluded not only that some symbols are of universal significance, but also that symbolism plays an important part in the psychic processes that influence every aspect of human thought and endeavour.

Jung believed the human psyche – the sum of conscious and unconscious mental activity – to have a real and discernible structure. Consciousness comprises the thoughts and actions under the control of the will. It is underlaid by the *preconscious*, the mental faculties and memories which can be readily summoned into consciousness, and by the *personal unconscious*, a vast reservoir of individual memories (perceptions, experiences and repressed desires) to which we occasionally gain access as they surface into consciousness through dreams or sudden flashes of recollection. Buried still deeper in the human psyche is the *collective unconscious*, the seat of those instinctive patterns of thought and behaviour that millennia of human experience have shaped into what we now recognize as emotions and values. These primordial images cannot be called up into consciousness: they can only be examined in symbolic form, personalized as men or women, or as images projected by our minds on to the outside world. Jung called these primordial symbols *archetypes*, and believed them to be the common inheritance of all men and women.

According to Jung, an individual is psychologically "healthy" when the conscious and unconscious minds are in dynamic balance. He held that psychic energy (the "life-force") flowed from the unconscious to the conscious to satisfy the demands of the conscious mind, and in the reverse direction to satisfy the unconscious mind. Any interruption of this *progression* or *regression* is a failure to reconcile the opposing forces that make up the human psyche, and leads to inner conflict. As well as the division between the conscious and the unconscious themselves, these forces consist of other "opposites", such as intuition and rationality, emotion and thought, instincts and spirituality, and the various paired aspects of the personality such as

Carl Gustav Jung
Born in Kesswil, Switzerland, on July 26, 1875, Jung grew up in an atmosphere dominated by the traditions of the Swiss Church. His father and eight uncles were all clergymen, and Jung himself seemed destined to become a minister. In his early years, Jung struggled to explain God and human existence in terms of the Christian faith, but became dissatisfied with the answers offered (particularly because his own father's belief was faltering). Jung's restless and inquiring mind drew him to the philosophy of Plato, Pythagoras and Heraclitus, which contributed to his decision to study medicine and psychiatry. He attended the University of Basle, and in 1900 joined the staff of the Burgholzli Mental Hospital, Zurich, where his work with association tests gained him an international reputation.

Jung's friendship with Sigmund Freud – the inventor of psychoanalysis – began in 1907, and for a period of five years the two collaborated closely and Jung held a number of important positions in the psychanalytic movement. However, Jung became increasingly critical of Freud's approach, and focused his attention on the description of psychological types (it was Jung who first coined the terms "introvert" and "extrovert") and the exploration of the collective unconscious through myth and symbolism. This historical approach helped Jung to develop a system of psychotherapy particularly suited to elderly and middle-aged patients whose lives had lost their meaning.

Jung spent much of the remainder of his life studying his own and his patients' unconscious material, analysing the myths and symbols of diverse cultures, and building up his own psychological theories. He died in Kusnacht, Switzerland, in 1961.

extroversion and introversion, mastery and sympathy, and negativity and conformity. Jung's realization that archetypal symbols can be used to explore the boundaries between the conscious and unconscious mind, had an important influence on his clinical techniques. He analysed the symbols generated in the dreams of his patients, seeing them as vital clues to their psychological problems and as indicators of their progress to recovery. Jung's techniques are widely used in psychotherapy today: for example, the patient may be encouraged to meditate upon a symbol, or to provide word associations with it in an attempt to unlock its meaning. Once this meaning becomes clear, the patient not only obtains new insights into his or her own mind, but usually finds that meaningful symbols begin to occur with greater and greater frequency, as if each symbol unlocks a door into the unconscious through which other symbols are then allowed to emerge.

It was largely because of his ideas on symbolism that Jung was forced to break with his friend and mentor, Sigmund Freud. Freud also attached great importance to the use of symbols in understanding the human mind, but took them to represent repressed sexuality or other definitive mental content. For example, anything that is erect or can be erected, or can penetrate, is regarded in Freudian theory as a symbol of the male sex organs, while anything that can be entered or penetrated is a symbol of the female. Freud identified countless symbols for both male and female genitalia, ranging from church steeples to billiard cues for the male, and from caves to handbags for the female. To use Jung's terminology, Freud saw symbols only as signs – concrete expressions of a known reality. However, to Jung, male and female sexuality were themselves only expressions of deeper creative forces. Thus, even though the intellect may tell us that a symbol is manifestly sexual, it is possible to go beyond this interpretation and discover within the symbol a further breadth of diversity and implication, and a metaphoric and enigmatic portrayal of psychic forces.

Jung and the Alchemists
The occurrence of alchemical symbols in the dreams and fantasies of his patients led Jung to believe that these symbols were powerful expressions of archetypal energies. Jung saw the development of religious belief as an ongoing process necessary for the growth of human consciousness, in which alchemical works were especially significant because they exposed the collective unconscious.

The Archetypes

The human race has always used symbols to express its awareness of the dynamic, creative forces underlying existence – variously believed to be the elements, the gods or the cosmos. At a more conscious level, symbols, particularly symbolic stories such as myths and legends, have been used to express abstract qualities, such as truth, justice, heroism, mercy, wisdom, courage and love. In Jungian terms, we are all born with instinctive predispositions toward these qualities, a set of internal blueprints of what it means to be fully human. These blueprints, or archetypes, have a dynamic aspect: they can be thought of as bundles of psychic energy that influence the manner in which we understand and react to life, and through which we develop motives, ideals, and certain facets of personality. Although they reside deep within the unconscious, the archetypes can be stimulated to emerge into consciousness, where they express themselves in the form of symbols and symbol systems.

According to Jung, we move toward psychological health when we recognize and reconcile our conflicting archetypal energies. This can be achieved through psychotherapy, by the careful study of dream symbolism, or alternatively by using symbols themselves as the point of departure. Instead of waiting for the archetypal symbols to emerge from the unconscious, existing symbols can be used as a focus for meditation, and thus provide pathways into the unconscious. The quest for self-knowledge through symbols is not the exclusive territory of Jungian psychology: to know oneself is an aspect of the enlightenment of which all the great philosophical and religious traditions speak. In the Gospel of Saint Philip, an early Christian text discovered at Nag in Egypt, Christ is recorded as saying: "Truth did not come into the world naked, but it came in types and images. One will not receive truth in any other way ... The bridegroom must enter through the image into the truth."

Identifying the Archetypes

From the knowledge gained from clinical studies and surveys of myth and tradition, Jung identified the main archetypal influences on human thought and behaviour. The *anima* is the female archetype, the collective, universal image of woman embedded in the male unconscious. It manifests itself as sentimentality and a tendency toward moodiness, compassion and tenderness (in Chinese folklore, a man in a bad mood was said to be exhibiting his feminine soul). The anima appears symbolically in legends and dreams as the princess imprisoned in a tower or the mysterious enchantress weaving magic spells. In its negative aspect, the anima can appear as the heartless, calculating female who lures a man, only to reject him when he is hopelessly ensnared. The *animus,* the collective image of man in the female unconscious, emerges symbolically as the ideal of manhood – the hero in shining armour, the adventurer who becomes a prince or overcomes the forces of evil – or in its negative aspect as the cruel, destructive man who treats a woman as a sex object and discards her once he has robbed her of her virginity and grown bored with her. It is the side of woman that is aggressive, power-seeking and opinionated.

Although they reflect universal patterns in the psyche, the animus and anima are shaped by, and themselves shape, individual experience. For example, a boy who has a poor relationship with his mother may relate his unconscious to the predominantly negative image of woman, or anima. Aspects of this anima may later be projected on to his future relationships with women, or may affect his psychological well-being in other, less direct ways. Similarly, in the process of falling in love, a woman may (often against her rational judgment and contrary to the advice of her friends) project onto the male all the qualities of strength and gallantry that reside in her animus.

Powerful processes are also at work with the other archetypes. While the *mother* archetype, the nurturing, caring side of human nature, begins to express itself from birth in a child's suckling and attachment behaviour, the *father* archetype typically emerges later (studies show that a child prefers a woman's voice to a man's in the early months of life). The father is the lord over the material, temporal world, while the mother is the ruler of the unseen world of emotions and feelings. In its positive aspect the father archetype is the protective presence, the wise king of legend, the just law-giver and judge. In his negative aspect he is the tyrant, the evil monster, the god Cronos who devours his own children.

Two other important archetypes are the *trickster* and the *shadow.* The former is the rebellious energy in psychological life, which enjoys denying or questioning the status quo, throwing a spanner into the smoothest machinery, and even in the midst of triumphs laughing at our achievements and prophesizing future disaster. The trickster has no obvious morals, is bound by no consistent code beyond its urge to disrupt and ridicule. At worst the trickster can destroy our self-confidence and overturn our most cherished beliefs, but it can also serve positive ends, prodding us out of complacency

The Animus
The character of a woman's animus – the male aspect of her psyche – is strongly influenced by the contact she has with men (especially her father) during her life, and often changes as a woman develops psychologically. In her early years the animus is typically embodied as an intensely physical, athletic man. It then becomes a man of action and initiative, a romantic figure (the "knight in shining armour") onto whom youthful desires are projected. In later life the animus becomes a benchmark of objective reality – the bearer of "the word", often personified as a spiritual leader or father-figure.

The Anima

The anima – the embodiment of female elements of the male psyche – appears in myth as goddess, prostitute, fairy or witch. In its negative aspect, the anima is often personified as a seductress who uses her wiles to bring about a man's humiliation or demise. It is here embodied in Salome, the biblical figure who persuaded Herod to behead John the Baptist by enchanting him with her dance.

In its positive aspect the anima is credited with spiritual powers and the hidden wisdom of the earth, elements and oceans: these characteristics of the anima are projected on to ships (which are traditionally feminine) and incorporated into ships' figureheads.

The Mother
In myths and legends the mother appears in the guise of Mother Nature, the bountiful earth mother, the various goddesses of fertility, or even nurturing animals such as the cow or she-wolf. The destructive side of the mother archetype (the hand that feeds can also withhold) also features in myth, for example as the terrifying Lilith of Hebrew mythology who appears as a demon that attacks men and children at night, or as the she-bear who drives away her young and leaves them to starve in the wilderness.

and forcing a re-examination of our goals. In myth, the trickster is best symbolized by the Norse god Loki, who variously helped or tricked the other gods, depending on whim.

The shadow is also disruptive energy, but of a different kind. It is the self-willed, self-seeking part of human nature, which in Western morality is looked upon as unequivocally evil. Projected outward, the shadow is the urge to find a scapegoat and to victimize those least able to defend themselves. But it also has a positive role, setting up a creative tension with the positive, sustaining, archetypal aspects within us, giving us something to "push against" in life, an inner obstacle to overcome. Although the shadow is an essential part of the psyche (in Western superstition, the man with no shadow is the devil himself), we commonly repress it during the early years of life, in the process of socialization, to be more worthy of our parents' love. Accepting the shadow in later life requires considerable moral effort and giving up some of our cherished ideals.

The Shadow

The shadow is an expression of the base, antisocial desires of which we are ashamed and attempt to bury in the unconscious: it is the inner terror that we feel might impel us to dark deeds should we ever lose our tight control over it. At its worst, the shadow is responsible for the cruelties that people have inflicted upon each other since the dawn of history. It is personified, in this 16th-century Indian painting, by the giant Zammurrad, who is forced to remain in a well. The shadow is also embodied by Satan and Ahriman (the evil spirit in the doctrine of Zoroastrianism). In modern legend it is Faust, who grew bored with his academic life and made a pact with the devil; or Dr Jekyll, whose own potion turned him into the evil Mr Hyde.

Cultural Perspectives

Jung's ideas on symbolism go only part of the way in accounting for the rich and varied symbolic vocabularies of different cultures. Assuming that the most powerful symbols arise from archetypes – aspects of the collective unconscious – why are their uses and meanings not consistent across cultural boundaries? For example, the genitalia are never used symbolically in Christian art, but in the East they are revered spiritual symbols. In the West, a fat belly is a symbol of gluttony, whereas to the Chinese it is an attribute of Shen Yeh, the god of wealth; in India it is associated with Ganesha, the elephant god of sacred wisdom; and to the Japanese it represents energy and knowledge. Even colours can carry different symbolic meanings: yellow, which in northern Europe connotes deceit and cowardice, is the imperial colour in China; in Buddhist tradition, yellow stands for humility and renunciation; while in the Mayan civilization of Central America, it was associated with the West.

The underlying reason for these differences is that the symbols used to portray archetypal energies are subject to the creative limitations of the human mind. Two individuals looking at the same clouds will see in them different shapes; similarly, it is rare for two people to hold an identical opinion of a third. In each case the stimulus is the same, but the response made to it depends upon the observer. At the cultural level, this process of differentiation receives further stimuli from the natural environment. For example, in parts of the arid Middle East sand came to symbolize purity, since it was used for washing in place of water, but in the wetter countries of Europe it became associated with instability and impermanence. The identities of a culture's gods – often the embodiments of Jungian archetypes – were also shaped by environment. The Norse gods displayed the qualities needed to survive in a cold, harsh climate – ferocity, determination, extroversion and intense physicality. However, the Hindu gods, though still representing the same archetypes, were more subtle and spiritualized, reflecting the slower pace of life on the Indian subcontinent.

Human nature thrives upon opposition and difference. Ethnic groups living close to each other often deliberately exaggerated small variations in the attributes of gods and goddesses into major discrepancies, each group claiming a right to an exclusive truth. When one race or one religion overcame another, it either absorbed the gods of the defeated group, adapting them to fit its own beliefs and iconography, or anathematized them. When Christianity came to Europe, it largely supplanted the pagan

The Scarab
The symbolic significance of animals and plants is associated with their distribution, and usually reflects some aspect of their behavioural and growth habits. The scarab, or dung beetle, was a powerful symbol in the civilizations of the Eastern Mediterranean, and particularly in ancient Egypt, where it was (mistakenly) believed to lay its eggs in balls of dung which it rolled into its nest. It therefore came to represent renewal and regeneration and, later, the endurance of the human soul. Dead beetles are often found in Egyptian tombs, and carved stone scarabs were used as amulets and as seals.

religions through systematically persecuting their adherents. On the other hand, when Buddhism arrived in Tibet in the 7th century AD, by invitation of King Sangsten Campo, it incorporated many of the symbols and practices of the indigenous shamanistic Bon religion, and converted some of the native deities into Buddhist bodhisattvas and lesser divinities. This is apparent when one compares the rich symbology of Tibetan Buddhism with the restraint of the earlier forms of Buddhism practised in Sri Lanka and in Southeast Asia.

Finally, symbols often become modified with the passage of time. As a culture advances, there is a tendency to regard the beliefs of previous generations as primitive or superstitious. Their symbols are rationalized and sanitized (in the way that company logos sometimes incorporate ancient symbols in their designs), interpreted literally, or simply abandoned altogether by the cultural elite (as has happened with a great deal of religious and mystical symbolism in the scientific West). Stripped from their context, such symbols diminish in power and have to be rediscovered afresh, just as Jung rediscovered the power of archetypal symbols when his patients spontaneously generated them in their dreams, and in their sketches and paintings.

The Dragon
The dragon carries opposite connotations in Orient and Occident. In the West it symbolizes mankind's basic, primeval nature, which must be vanquished by strength and self-discipline, and in Christian myth it embodies the forces of the underworld and Satan. In the East, however, the dragon is seen as a symbol of joy, dynamism, good health and fertility, and its image is believed to ward off evil spirits. In China, depictions of dragons holding pearls (left) – symbols of thunder – were thought to bring about rain.

The Power of Symbols

Symbols tend to accumulate their meanings slowly, over hundreds of years. Like languages, their connotations proliferate along many branches, dividing, following a variety of distinctive routes according to the cultural context, sometimes doubling back on themselves along lines of influence. However, some symbols, or types of symbols, are so universally potent, so close to the very stuff of life, that their meanings tend to remain constant or to vary within a much narrower spectrum.

Unsurprisingly, there is often a connection between the power of symbols and their antiquity. Primitive societies inhabited a world where the most basic requirements of life – warmth, food, shelter, fire, sunshine, rain, sex – loomed large. Alongside the instinct to survive and reproduce was the instinct to find meanings, to make more sense of the necessities on which life depended. The sun, we presume, was an object of intense speculation, and certainly in due course became the theme of some of our most powerful myths. If the sun was crucial to life, then perhaps the stars were too; and from this perspective, it is not too difficult to understand the evolution of astrology. As civilizations developed over the centuries, these early preoccupations retained their force, and even today, in the most affluent of cultures, the symbols connected with them lodge in the mind and resonate with power.

In the present age, although the rational still takes precedence over the numinous in most aspects of public life, at a personal level we still believe that profound realities dwell beyond the reach of objective reason. We are ready to acknowledge that such truths are eternal, and we sense instinctively that the language of symbolism will give us access to them. This in part explains why even ancient symbols seem full of potential energy, as if addressing some hidden centre within ourselves.

Such powerful, far-reaching connotations are the theme of the following section, which traces the development of symbols in religion, myth, ritual, prayer and magic, and looks at some key themes in the language of symbolism.

Paleolithic Art in the Lascaux Caves

Sometimes referred to as the "Sistine Chapel of Paleolithic art" the Lascaux grotto contains probably the finest existing display of prehistoric painting. Hundreds of individual images cover the walls of the main cave and its several connecting galleries: many of the paintings are high on the walls of the cave, and their completion would have required some form of scaffolding. The artists who worked in the caves are thought to have been "professionals" within their communities, because many of the animal paintings are anatomically accurate and well executed, employing innovative artistic devices to convey perspective.

The cave is thought to have been the site of primitive initiation rituals. This theory is substantiated by the observations of the first archaeologists to examine the cave, who found the footprints of children and young adults in the darkest recesses of the labyrinth.

Symbols in Prehistory

The ability to devise, manipulate and comprehend symbols at an abstract level is one of the main characteristics that distinguish mankind from our primate relatives. Logic, creativity and aesthetics all arise from this ability, which is the cornerstone of the anthropological notion of "culture". The earliest known manifestations of this unique human attribute are the cave paintings of the Paleolithic Period (the Old Stone Age), some of which are more than 30,000 years old.

Paleolithic people were nomadic hunter-gatherers, whose needs for food and clothing were met largely by game – deer, mammoths, wild oxen and horses. They were attracted to rock overhangs and cave openings, in which they pitched their skin tents, but archaeological evidence suggests that they did not live in the interiors of caves, which were dark, wet and unstable. The most celebrated Paleolithic paintings are found deep in the labyrinthine cave systems of Lascaux (France) and Altamira (Spain), suggesting that this primitive art was not intended to be viewed, and that its function was not merely decorative. Many anthropologists now believe that cave paintings were of profound symbolic significance to our distant ancestors, and that the cave itself was a sacred place of initiation, representing the womb of the earth or the home of the spirits who ruled the primitive imagination.

The symbols encountered in cave paintings fall into two main categories – naturalistic depictions of animals, and abstract, sometimes geometric, forms, such as quadrangles, spirals and groups of dots or lines. Interpretations of these symbols are highly speculative. The animal paintings sometimes show a shaman leaping high above horses, bison and mammoths. Early anthropological studies took these paintings to be a form of sympathetic magic arising from a belief that the depiction of success in the hunt would be translated into reality. Later explanations, however, held that the spatial arrangements of animal images within the caves were of cosmological significance, reflecting the patterns in which Paleolithic peoples ordered their world.

The abstract symbols of prehistoric peoples are particularly intriguing because they show little variation in form over a period of 20,000 years. This extraordinary continuity, unique in art history, suggests that they were of great significance. However, the meanings of these symbols remain unclear. They may have served a calendric or magical function, or they may have expressed fundamental patterns in the human psyche. The latter explanation is superficially attractive: a recurring motif in Paleolithic art is a

The Power of Masks
In many primitive societies, to wear a mask was to invoke a supernatural being. In Africa, masks were used to ward off enemies, to summon ancestors, and in rituals and ceremonies that marked alliances between tribes. Masks, particularly those depicting animals, were also used as a means of denying personal identity, thereby bringing the wearer closer to the paradisal state.

The Gods of Ancient Egypt
Many ancient Egyptian gods, traditions
and cults had their roots in prehistoric
African beliefs. Certain animals were
considered to be the sacred manifestations
of the gods on earth. For example, the ibis
was thought to embody qualities of Thoth,
the god of wisdom. Ibises were often
embalmed and entombed with deceased
kings in the belief that they would confer
wisdom in the after-life.

The Symbolism of the Elements
In the ancient world, the elements (air,
earth, water, fire) were believed to be
under the control of the gods. In Aztec
tradition, the gods periodically destroyed
the world by unleashing upon it a different
elemental force, before recreating it in a
new form. The destructive power of the
elements is used also as a symbol of divine
punishment for human shortcomings. The
symbolism of the flood features in the
myths of many cultures, but is probably
best known from the biblical story of the
Great Flood, where Noah's ark (right)
represents salvation through the Church.

group of seven dots or parallel lines, and the number seven is universally considered to be sacred, even to this day (see page 64).

Lacking scientific knowledge, the early peoples responded to the natural world at an intuitive level. They may have believed (as did later cultures) that consciousness was shared by all things, animate and inanimate alike, and that this consciousness could be addressed through symbols. From this belief sprang rituals such as the rain dance, in which the sound of rain falling on the ground was imitated by the stamping of feet, and the fertility dances, which were thought to induce the return of life in the spring. The prominent place of fertility in ancient symbol systems is also apparent from what archaeologists call Venus sculptures – small ivory or stone figures of large-breasted women. Found from Europe's Altantic coast right across to Siberia, these figures symbolized fertility in all its aspects, and were probably the forerunners of the earth-mother cults of early European civilization.

By the Neolithic Period (the New Stone Age, around 10,000 years ago) people had adopted a more sedentary existence, living in larger communities, and modifying and cultivating the land to suit their requirements. This change in lifestyle prompted the development of more organized public rituals, which embraced virtually all aspects of life. For example, archaeological evidence (pottery, food and ornaments found in contemporary funeral mounds) points to the proliferation of funerary symbolism in the Neolithic. Death was regarded as a journey, on which the deceased (the travellers) were symbolically accompanied by essential provisions and treasured possessions. It was also believed that by dying symbolically (entering a trance, or being symbolically dismembered), a shaman, priest or priestess could journey to the land of the dead to converse with the spirits, and return to the world of the living in a state of esoteric wisdom. Trance states were used in this way by later cultures: they appear in Dionysian cults of ancient Greece and among the native tribes of North America.

The Totem Pole
Among the native North Americans of the northwest coast of the United States and Canada, the totem pole had a function similar to that of the heraldic emblem in medieval Europe. The animals, spirits or other symbolic forms carved into its length signified the identity of a family or tribe, or served as a pictorial account of their history. Totem poles were also used as grave markers, and as decorative elements in the structure of houses.

Gods and Myths

There are no more powerful symbols than the gods themselves. They are capable of arousing intense emotion and unlocking stores of energy that have, over the centuries, fuelled both the highest art and the bloodiest battles. In Jungian terms, the gods, and the myths that set out their relationship with mankind, are conscious expressions of unconscious, archetypal energies (see page 13). The deities and their associated symbols actually emerge from, and are given form within, our own psychological lives, but they address the unconscious at such a profound level that they *appear* to come from some spiritual source outside ourselves. They are, according to Jung, embodiments of mankind's "natural religious function", an aspect of the psyche that must be developed to ensure psychic health and stability.

If this explanation sounds as if it reduces the gods – or God – to figments of our collective imagination, nothing could be further from the truth. For it does not deny that the collective unconscious may be in communication with an even deeper substratum of reality, one which represents the true creative source of our individual lives. What Jungians say is that we must recognize that this source, when discovered, can only reveal itself to us in a symbolic form. As the Bible tells us, we cannot look upon the face of God and live. We can only know him in a limited, and limiting, symbolic form.

Although they originate in the human psyche, the gods of most cultures have been externalized, their energies projected on to the outside world, in order to make their presence more immediate and tangible. In the Hindu pantheon, for example, Brahma represents the creative power that brings the universe into being; Vishnu the sustaining power that preserves and protects; and Shiva the forces of change. And in ancient Egypt, the gods were symbolized by animals that best exemplified their powers. Thus, the falcon, soaring high into the heavens and with a sharpness of vision from which nothing can hide, symbolized the god Horus, lord of the sky; the frog, with its great fecundity, symbolized Heket, the goddess of birth; the cow represented Hathor, the mother goddess; and the crocodile stood for Ammit, who gobbles up the hearts of those laden with sin.

The Role of Myth

Myths are symbolic narratives – tales of gods, humans with superhuman powers, and extraordinary events – that were once of central importance in all cultures. It was through these allegorical tales that a society could establish and explore its identity; and, in many cultures, myths provided a

The Gods of the Aztec Calendar
Originally from northern Mexico, the Aztecs settled around Lake Texcoco in central Mexico in the 12th century. Over the next four centuries they built up a powerful empire based on intensive agriculture. Aztec religion and myth incorporated elements from the cultures they subdued or absorbed, and their pantheon was accordingly large and diverse. The gods were closely entwined with the complex Aztec calendar, which combined two cycles – a solar cycle of 365 days and a ritual cycle of 260 days. The latter was divided into 13 periods of 20 days, in which each day was governed by a particular deity, who determined fate on that day. Images of the gods, such as that above, were used by Aztec priests in calendrical divination.

The Avatars of Vishnu
In Hindu tradition, Vishnu – the protector of the world, mankind and *dharma* (moral order) – is worshipped as one of the major deities. He is known through his ten avatars (descents into the world), which are forms assumed by Vishnu to fight a particular form of evil. Vishnu took the form of a fish to warn Manu, humanity's earliest ancestor, of an imminent deluge. He sent Manu a large ship, ordering him to load it with two of every living species and the seeds of all plants. Manu had just completed his task when the ocean submerged all the land. In this way, Vishnu saved all life from destruction.

Eos, Goddess of the Dawn
The elements, the weather and the
movements of celestial bodies were often
attributed to the gods. The myths of many
cultures were concerned with the exploits
and relationships of these deities, and
through them make sense of otherwise
inexplicable phenomena. The Greeks
personified dawn as the goddess Eos: every
morning, she stole away from the bed of
her husband, Tithonus, emerged from the
ocean and rose into the sky on a chariot
drawn by two horses. The morning dew
was her tears of grief for her son Memnon,
who was killed by Achilles.

stylized model for human behaviour. From his studies of the Amerindian
peoples of North and South America, the French anthropologist Claude
Lévi-Strauss suggested that the purpose of myth was to provide a logical
model capable of explaining life's apparent contradictions. By comparing
and contrasting opposing facets of existence – night and day, hunger and
satiation, unity and diversity – in narrative form, the myth-makers were
able to make sense of the world around them. Although this interpretation
accounts for some components of myth, it cannot fully explain all the
various ways in which myth is observed to function in society.

Some myths explain the state of things, as in the numerous North
American myths that describe the origins of corn, or give meaning to the rituals practiced by a particular group of people. In Syria, the myth of the triumph of Baal (the god of fertility) over his enemies was acted out in rituals
designed to ensure the parallel triumph of fertility over the barrenness of the
earth. Other myths account for the creation of the world or of mankind: for
example, in the creation myth of the Shilluk people of the Sudan, Juok (God)
makes man from clay. He travels north to find white clay, from which he
fashions Europeans, and uses black earth to make the African people. He
gives people long legs to let them run in the shallows while fishing and long
arms with which to swing hoes. The creation myth of the Carabaulo people
of Timor includes a justification of the social order: it relates that the ancestors of the island's present population emerged from a vulva-shaped hole in
the ground: first to emerge were the landowning aristocrats, followed by the
commoners and tenants. Similarly, the ruling families of many ancient civilizations – from Egypt to Imperial China – invoked myths of divine origin to
legitimize their position.

Myths also address the question of mortality (in some myths death is
interpreted as a divine mistake) and describe the ultimate fate of the individual self: the Egyptian *Book of the Dead*, a collection of magical and religious
texts dating back to the 16th century BC, chronicles the symbolic passage of
the soul through the after-life in meticulous detail, giving precise instructions on how the departed must meet each of the challenges and opportunities which he or she will find there.

Freud saw myth as society's way of giving vent to repressed ideas and
experiences. For example, he considered that the repressed erotic feelings of
a son for his mother and the associated feelings of antipathy toward his
father, emerged in the myth of Oedipus. In Greek legend, Oedipus was a

Ma-Ku
In Chinese mythology, Ma-Ku was a benificent sorceress who personified the goodness in all people. In her first avatar (pictured left), she reclaimed a large tract of land from the sea and planted it with mulberry trees. In another incarnation, Ma-Ku tricked her cruel father into giving his slaves more rest. Her father became violently angry and Ma-Ku fled to become a hermit. Her father was overcome with remorse and went blind through weeping: Ma-Ku returned to comfort her father and bathe his eyes with a curative potion.

Theban hero who unwittingly killed his father, Laius, and married his mother, Jocasta: upon realizing what he had done, he blinded himself. For Freud, the myth expressed the collective guilt of humanity at having harboured such feelings toward its progenitors.

In Jungian psychology, myths are symbolic journeys through life, and their protagonists are embodiments of unconscious archetypes. For example, in myths narrating the deeds of heroes, the hero is taken to symbolize the ego, and the stories relate how the hero becomes aware of his strengths and weaknesses (develops his ego-awareness). Once the hero is master of his ego, he dies, usually through an act of self-sacrifice, which symbolizes his passing into maturity. In many myths the hero is guided by an advisor or tutor, who in Jungian terms corresponds to the whole psyche, the complete human identity, which provides the resources that the ego itself lacks.

Ritual, Magic and Prayer

Rites and rituals are an important feature of all societies, past and present. They help to maintain the integrity of a community and prepare each individual for the role he or she is expected to play within it. Not surprisingly, rituals are most prominent in small, close-knit tribal groups, although they persist in Western cities, where, for example, baptism, marriage and funerary rites are still generally respected.

Rituals are physical enactments of spiritual journeys – or, in Jungian terms, journeys into the collective unconscious – in which the body is taken as the symbol of the spirit. They can symbolize progression toward enlightenment or the gods (the ritual dances of the ancient Mesopotamians, for example, symbolically imitated the journey of the goddess Ishtar to the underworld), or the journey of death and subsequent rebirth, in which we sacrifice our identity and pass renewed into the next stage of life. In many religions, rituals mirror the supposed order in the sacred realm, and thus establish a closer link between the human and divine worlds. The Roman Catholic Church, for example, holds that the seven sacraments – baptism, confirmation, the eucharist, penance, holy orders, matrimony and extreme unction – were instituted by Christ himself. Numerous religions have purification rituals in which bodily pollution, which is thought to be offensive to the gods, is removed. A polluted body (one that had been in contact with disease, death or sin) could be symbolically cleansed by bathing in a fast-flowing stream or in blood (which is associated with both life and death, and therefore stands for renewal), or in rituals using weapons or firecrackers to fight off evil spirits symbolically.

In tribal societies, initiation rituals were used to mark the passage from boyhood into adulthood. They often involved the deliberate infliction of pain (such as circumcision or tattooing), trials of strength and endurance, or a lengthy period of fasting, in order to add a physical dimension to the symbolic invocation of death and rebirth. Similarly, a young girl would pass into maturity through fertility rites involving movement and dance or through symbolic beatings that represented her passivity and submission to the physical demands of womanhood (menstruation, pregnancy and child rearing). These rites of passage involve an irrevocable break with the childhood world, during which, according to Jung, the parental archetypes are damaged (through symbolic death) and the ego is consolidated with the larger group (often represented by a totem – an animal or object that embodies tribal unity). Marriage is another type of initiation ritual. As in the rites of passage

Funerary Rites in Ancient Egypt
The ancient Egyptians developed elaborate funerary rituals in the belief that the immortal soul of the deceased maintained links with this world through the entombed body. The body was preserved indefinitely through mummification, and provided with food and offerings to sustain it in the next world.

In Egyptian belief, the deceased was ceremonially judged by a panel of divinities, including Anubis (the Jackal-headed god of embalming) and Thoth (the ibis-headed god of wisdom), and presided over by Osiris, the lord of the underworld. The heart of the deceased, which was believed to be the seat of the emotions, was weighed against a feather, a symbol of justice (above). If the two balanced, the dead man or woman passed into the blessed after-life. On failing the test, the deceased was devoured by Ammit, a fearsome hybrid beast – part crocodile, part lion, part hippopotamus.

described above, it uses tatooes, rings and special garments to signify new social status. The ritual itself often involves a symbolic acting out of the new responsibilities of both partners to each other and to their families. For the man in particular, marriage represents a loss of independence – in Jungian terms, the sacrifice of the hero archetype – which in some cultures is offset by the symbolic abduction or rape of the bride.

The idea of sacrifice as a way of bringing about renewal also lay behind the fertility rituals carried out in the short winter days to ensure the return of life in the spring. Just as the earth had to die in winter to ensure rebirth into the fruitfulness of summer, so the king – or, more likely, someone who had been named king for the occasion – had to die in order to ensure that his people would live. The Aztecs believed that without offerings of human blood and hearts, the sun would cease to shine and the universe would cease to exist. Ritual sacrifice therefore featured prominently in Aztec culture, to the extent that all wars were officially waged for the purpose of obtaining sacrificial victims (although their actual goals were undoubtedly more mercenary).

The belief that nature and the will of the gods could be influenced by rituals and symbols was also the fundamental principle of magic. The magician's aim was to move progressively through the planes that were thought to make up existence, eventually to merge into the ineffable reality from which, in mortal life, men and women stand exiled. In raising himself (or herself) toward the gods, the magician had a responsibility to influence them in beneficial ways. In all occult systems, from the Egyptian and Greek mysteries to the native American tradition and the work of the European alchemists and Kabbalists, the true magician was engaged on a serious quest which had nothing to do with personal power or ill will toward others.

Prayer may be a personal or collective act of communication with the sacred. In either case, it is often surrounded by symbolism and ritual. In most religions, bodily posture and the position of the hands indicate submission and homage. Objects are sometimes used to focus prayer or to continue supplication to the god while the supplicant is asleep or otherwise occupied: in Buddhism, for example, the mantra on a prayer flag is believed to be activated by the wind. The Islamic devotional prayer, the *salat,* is governed by ritual. It is performed five times a day, as it was during Muhammad's lifetime, and is preceded by rites of ablution. During the prayer, the faithful face Mecca and execute the *rak'ahs,* the physical postures that accompany recitations from the Koran.

The Eucharist
The sacrament of the Eucharist is the central act of worship in the Christian faith. It involves the consecration of bread and wine (symbolically, figuratively or actually equated with the body and blood of Christ) and their distribution among the worshippers (communion). The sacrament is surrounded by esoteric symbolism: for example, the chalice that holds the wine (or blood) is, in Jungian terms, a spiritual womb. In this 16th-century symbolic depiction of Christ's passion, the chalice filled with blood is surrounded by three nails (traditionally the number used in the crucifixion of Christ).

Male and Female

Images of man and woman are of deep symbolic significance in their own right. In Jungian psychology they are thought to be conscious expressions of the *animus* and *anima* archetypes (see pages 13–15), and in many cultures they appear together as symbols of fertility and the endless renewal of life. At a more esoteric level, the theme of masculinity and femininity can take on different connotations. Taken separately, man and woman symbolize incompleteness: each is barren and unfruitful, one half of a preexisting whole. It is as if the first, universal human being had been cleaved in two at some point in the unknowable past, and was doomed to go through history suffering the anguish of separation, constantly longing to be reunited with the lost half of the self.

This theme reveals itself in numerous myths and legends, from Isis and Osiris to Orpheus and Eurydice, in which man and woman struggle against overwhelming odds to be united. In the legend of Tristram and Isolde, the lovers achieve true oneness only after their deaths, when two trees grow from their graves, and their branches intertwine so that they can never be parted. In the cosmologies of the ancients, heaven and earth (which were believed to have once been united) were often depicted as man and woman: in ancient Egypt, heaven was personified as the goddess Nut and earth as the god Geb.

Even when man and woman come together in the act of love, their union remains ultimately incomplete. Limited by the constraints of the human body, it stops short of a full merging of the lovers. Thus, many of the major spiritual and occult traditions have taught that completion can be achieved only internally, in the union of the male and female principles that we each carry within us – the opposing creative forces of active and passive. In the East, this idea of inner union finds expression in the Tai Chi symbol (see page 129), and in Hindu and Buddhist Tantra, where the male and female deities are shown entwined in an embrace so intricate that the two appear to inhabit a single body. Western occult and alchemical traditions embodied the attainment of inner reconciliation (and therefore of true wisdom) as the hermaphrodite (or androgyne), who is at once male and female. In Jewish legend, Adam himself was hermaphroditic until Eve was separated from him, and in some Greek accounts Zeus was simultaneously male and female. In shamanic religions, the male priest often dresses as a woman to recreate symbolically the state of primordial perfection that existed before the sexes were separated.

The Chemical Wedding
Alchemists thought of themselves as artists/scientists, whose strictly controlled chemical operations could bring nature to perfection (a process symbolized by the transformation of base metal into gold). The alchemist's vessel was a microcosm – a universe in miniature – in which this transformation took place. Alchemical operations were described in vividly symbolic terms, partly to ensure that their secrets did not fall into the wrong hands. A crucial stage in the process was the uniting of the male and female principles of matter, which was sometimes symbolized as a hermaphrodite (above) or the wedding between a king and queen.

Krishna and Radha

Krishna, the eighth avatar (incarnation) of Vishnu, is one of the most popular of all Hindu divinities. Numerous myths tell of his pranks and amorous exploits. It is said that as a young man, Krishna enchanted the *gopis* (milkmaids) in the region of Brindaban by playing the flute on autumn evenings, and lured the young women away from their sleeping husbands to dance ecstatically with him in the forest. Although each *gopi* thought Krishna to be her exclusive partner, he developed a deep love for Radha (above), whose golden beauty complemented Krishna's dark form (his name means "dark" or "dark as a cloud").

Opposition and Unity

All the great forces of nature and the human emotions have their opposites by which they are partly defined. Without light, there would be no concept of darkness; without sorrow, the experience of joy would be diminished; and without woman, there could be no man. Just as male and female can be unified at the esoteric level (see page 32), so can all opposites be reconciled to recreate the paradisal state. Many Eastern traditions hold that opposites arose when the one true reality fragmented into apparent disunity to create the world of forms (in the Hindu faith, it is said that "the one becomes two, the two become three, and from the three come the ten thousand things"): each fragment is incomplete in itself and longs to be reunited with the wholeness from which it came .

The Buddhist saying, "When the opposites arise, the Buddha-mind is lost", refers to the limitations of oppositional perception. By making sharp distinctions we are blinded to the fact that all opposites in reality spring from the same source, and that the whole of creation is in truth still one. The opposites, and the material world which they constitute, are a subjective reality, and the enlightened mind can see through this to the unity which is its true nature.

The unity underlying diversity, and the mutual interdependence of opposites, is expressed symbolically in numerous objects and shapes. The cup, for example, illustrates that form cannot exist without space, and vice-versa. The sides of the cup belong to the world of form, while the space they contain belongs to the world of emptiness. Form and space together are expressions of the fundamental unity of the cup. Symbols such as the circle illustrate wider aspects of this truth. Similarly, although we regard concepts such as "beginning" and "end" as opposites, each point on the circumference of a circle can be both a beginning and an end. Accordingly, in Zen Buddhism the circle stands for enlightenment and the perfection of humanity in unity with the primal principle, and the Chinese Tai Chi symbol (see page 129) is enclosed in a circle. At a more complex level, mandalas and yantras (see page 60) symbolize the illusory nature of observed differences, and their spontaneous appearance in meditation and across cultures suggests that, in the collective unconscious, we are aware of the truth which they represent. In Hinduism and Buddhism, it is said that "life and death are the same": this expresses the belief that even the two fundamental opposites – existence and non-existence – are mutually dependent, and are facets of the same unity.

Two Realms
Many cultures believed the cosmos to be divided into two realms – heavenly and earthly. The heavens were the home of the gods and higher powers, and were associated with spirit and intellect, while the earth was the place of matter and physicality. The organization of the earthly realm (microcosm) was held to mirror that of the heavens (macrocosm): the correspondence between macrocosm and microcosm is the subject of this 17th-century alchemical image (above). Mankind was believed to hold a unique position in the universe, having access to both realms.

Good and Evil

In this 18th-century print by William Blake, what appear to be good and evil angels struggle for posession of a child, a symbol of the lost innocence of undivided Man. Blake devised his own mythology to explore, through art and literature, his belief that Man's predicament resulted from his inability to reconcile the elements of his divided self. In terms of Blake's myth, the "good" angel is Los, a symbol of the imagination, while the "evil" angel is Orc, a symbol of energy and revolt. Blake believed that mankind's inner conflicts could be resolved through the imagination, rather than the intellect.

Cross-currents

When different peoples come into contact through trade, conflict or migration, their cultural signifiers – or symbols – rarely remain unchanged. The symbols of one group typically enrich, modify or supplant those of the other, and the resulting changes in artistic expression, myth and tradition bear lasting witness to the meeting of the two cultures. For example, the obvious parallels between the Roman and Greek pantheons are no accident. When they conquered Greece in the 3rd century AD, the Romans borrowed heavily from the richer, more developed mythology of the Greeks, and appended the characteristics of the Greek gods to their own deities. The Greek Dionysus was incorporated into the Roman Bacchus; and the myths surrounding Artemis, Zeus, Hermes and Aphrodite were projected onto Diana, Jupiter, Mercury and Venus respectively. A number of Greek gods, including Apollo, were even taken over in name as well as in function by the Romans, as were some of the Greek heroes, such as Herakles (Hercules).

A similar process of absorption occurred when Buddhism reached China along the silk trade route in the 1st century AD. Its fusion with the prevailing nature-oriented religion of Taoism resulted in Ch'an (which later developed in Japan into Zen Buddhism). Ch'an rejected the idea of worship through images, rites and rituals: nature was considered to be the symbol of ultimate reality, and awareness and experience of the natural world was held to be the true path to enlightenment.

The organized "export" of religion (and therefore of symbols) only began in earnest in the 4th century AD, following the adoption of Christianity as the official religion of Rome. Proselytizing from the outset, Christianity anathematized and actively suppressed all forms of paganism. But indigenous beliefs and symbols proved difficult to eradicate, and the Christians were forced to compromise, tacitly tolerating those symbols that could readily be Christianized, and recognizing others as partial statements of a spiritual reality that reached its final consummation in the coming of Christ. In particular, many of the legends surrounding the shadowy lives of the early Christian saints seem to be based on pre-Christian myths. Saint Christopher, who is usually depicted as a giant carrying the Christ-child across a river, echoes Charon, who in Greek myth was charged with ferrying the souls of the deceased over the river Styx. Saint Catherine of Alexandria, from whose veins milk was said to have flowed after her martyrdom, carries echoes of the Egyptian goddess Isis, one of whose attributes was milk.

From Egypt to Rome
The geographical migration of symbols is exemplified by this 1st-century fresco from the Villa of the Mysteries, Pompeii, which shows the Egyptian goddesses Isis and Nephthys flanking a sacred crocodile.

Christian and Pre-Christian Themes

Reverence for the Virgin Mary has pre-Christian origins in the cults of female divinities, such as that of Artemis and Diana, which were prominent among pre-Christian Mediterranean peoples. In this 13th-century painting, the crescent moon at the feet of Mary is a symbol borrowed from ancient Egypt, where it was an attribute of the goddess Isis, the Queen of Heaven.

The great festivals of the Christian calendar, such as Christmas and Easter, coincide with pagan festivals, and many of the objects closely associated with Christmas, such as the yule log, mistletoe, and the Christmas tree itself, were all borrowed from pre-Christian traditions.

The Uses of Symbols

Through the centuries, symbols, in their infinite variety, have enriched the life of the mind. Cultures in all parts of the world have developed and built upon an understanding of symbols and symbol systems to promote spiritual, bodily and intellectual well-being. The following section looks at three very different ways in which symbols could be said to be *used* by the mind or the imagination – art, meditation and dreaming.

Symbolism nourishes artistic endeavour both consciously and unconsciously. In many traditional cultures, much art is purely symbolic in content, expressing in visual terms the beliefs and aspirations of the community. In Western civilization, art began to lose some of its more explicit symbolic purpose with the rise of the notion of artistic individualism: symbolism, after all, is an essentially collective activity. However, there were various ways in which symbolism in art remained current – as an expression of archetypal themes; as a conscious exploitation of traditional imagery; or as a means of communicating private messages. In modern times, the interest in the workings of the mind has prepared the ground for a tradition of expressly symbolic art, which has continued to resist the enticements of abstraction.

Meditation reflects a deep-rooted belief, in many cultures, that discipline of the mind, correctly applied, can lead to a form of psychic, spiritual or bodily enhancement, or even to an ultimate reality that would otherwise be inaccessible. Getting in touch with the inner self, and silencing the distractions that disturb our peace, are dual aspects of the process. In mystical forms of meditation, symbols such as the wheel or lotus provide access to a higher reality.

Dream symbolism is a vast subject in itself, and in the section that follows we can do little more than generalize. Interpretation of dream symbolism is complicated by the need to take into account the individual circumstances and personality of the dreamer. Nevertheless, a knowledge of the Jungian archetypes is extremely helpful, and by recording and questioning our dreams over a period of time we can gain valuable insights into the messages they bring from the unconscious.

Symbols in Art

The history of art is a record of mankind's most moving and meaningful symbols. From the Paleolithic Period (see page 22) onward, artists have made use of esoteric and exoteric symbols to express the beliefs and preoccupations of their time. Artefacts of all civilizations bear witness to the intimate relationship between religion and symbolism. In ancient Egypt, stonemasons would inscribe statues of kings and noblemen with the names of their owners in the belief that the statues would provide eternal resting places for their spirits after death. Stelae (slabs of stone set up at the tombs of prominent Egyptians) had a similar function. Decorated with carvings showing the deceased beside a table laden with offerings to the gods, and inscribed with magical symbols and ritual prayers to Osiris (lord of the two worlds), they were designed to ensure the safety of the dead man's soul.

Although funerary and decorative art dating from the Bronze Age (3,000–1,100BC) has been found in Northern Europe, the most significant developments in Western art throughout this period took place in the flourishing towns and cities of the Mediterranean. The Minoan civilization of Crete, which owed a great deal to the earlier cultures of Egypt and Mesopotamia, made extensive use of spirals, wavy lines and other geometric motifs in its pottery and metalwork. It is believed that these symbols, which

The Annunciation
In this painting of the Annunciation (the announcement by the archangel Gabriel to the Virgin Mary that she would conceive a son by the Holy Spirit), Renaissance artist Domenico Venezianno uses the symbolism of colour and geometry to emphasize the momentousness of the occasion. The lily held by Gabriel is a Christian symbol of virginal love, innocence and the Virgin Mary. Its whiteness stands for her purity; its straight stalk her godliness; and its downward-curving leaves her humility.

echoed the sea and the elements, were expressions of a sense of shared existence with nature, and may also have been used in talismans to ensure safe passage for seafarers and travellers. Minoan frescoes often depicted rituals, religious ceremonies and battles, and frequently featured bulls, griffins and other animals, which may have had a symbolic protective value.

Following the demise of the great Minoan and Mycenaean kingdoms in the 13th century BC, the Greeks took over and refined the geometric style of the earlier cultures, and the symbolism of abstract forms – zigzag designs, triangles, meanders and swastikas – dominated Greek art for four centuries. It was not until the 8th century BC that symbolism in Greek art reached new levels of pictorial expression and clarity. At this time, stereotyped animals and human figures, rituals and battles began to appear as themes in ceramics and other artefacts; and narrative art, which chronicled the deeds of gods and heroes, began to emerge in the 7th century BC. The figures in these narratives were vivid embodiments of unconscious archetypes. In art, as well as in philosophy and myth, they symbolized the quest for self-knowledge and served as metaphors for all aspects of public and private life. Greek artists borrowed heavily from the cultures of Syria, Phoenicia and Egypt. Mythical creatures from the East – gorgons, chimeras and harpies – were Hellenized, becoming more elegant and less frightening. Moreover, Egyptian influence began to stimulate the creation of large, free-standing statues, which evolved in due course into the harmony and beauty of classical Greek sculpture.

A similar emphasis upon the visual power of symbols to alter consciousness is apparent in the art of India and the East. The erotic couplings of the Hindu gods symbolize the diversity of creation, as well as the Tantric techniques which allow sexual union to serve as a path to enlightenment. The lingam of Shiva (see page 125) symbolizes not only creative energy but also the number one (primal unity), while other erotic sculptures use sexuality to represent the joys of heaven, and eternal bliss. In painting, a common theme is Krishna's amorous adventures with the milkmaids, which symbolize the entry of divine love into the world, or the five universal pleasures embodied in meat, alcohol, grain, fish and sexual intercourse.

Chinese art has always been exalted of purpose, striving to inspire and educate the viewer, and provide insights into the nature of mankind and the Great Ultimate. Spiritual and moral messages were conveyed through certain "noble" themes, particularly landscapes and the natural world, which developed into highly stylized forms of symbolic expression. For example,

The Evangelists
Medieval depictions of the four Evangelists as man, lion, ox and eagle were inspired by the four creatures of Ezekiel, and by ancient Eastern symbolism, according to which this tetrad represented the four guardians of the earth, or the four supporters of the heavens.

every part of the landscape was held to symbolize an aspect of mankind: water was the blood of the mountains, grass and trees their hair, clouds and mists their clothing, while the solitary wandering scholar, who often featured in such paintings, was their soul. Bamboo represented the spirit of the scholar, which could be bent but not broken, and jade stood for purity. Such explicit symbolism was also a feature of Chinese architecture. For example, the curved gable-ends so typical of Chinese houses were not merely decorative devices, but were believed to launch demons back into space should they try to slide down the roof in an attempt to visit the occupants.

In medieval Europe, Christian icons – representations of Christ, the Virgin Mary and the saints – functioned as focal points of worship. Narrative paintings, with their multiple layers of symbolism, served to instruct the illiterate masses in the scriptures and the mysteries of the faith, and also to spell out mankind's relationship with God and the cosmos. In the Middle Ages the artistic devices used to express the essence of Christian faith emphasized the otherworldliness of God, the distance of the heavenly realm from the earth, and the idea that salvation could be achieved only through the elevation of the spirit. This mystical view of the universe was reflected in all forms of visual art and literature, but perhaps most spectacularly in the towering Gothic cathedrals, which were often made to appear higher still by the skilful manipulation of perspective.

The nature of Christian art and symbolism underwent fundamental change in the Renaissance. Growing rationalism and knowledge of the natural world, together with the reevaluation of Christian and classical texts, resulted in a greater naturalism in the visual arts. Nature, the human body and Greco-Roman myth once again became respectable themes in religious painting and sculpture. For example, in his famous painting of the Last Judgement, Michaelangelo cast Christ in the role of Apollo or Hercules rather than portraying him as crucified saviour. Similarly, in the Raphael Loggia in the Vatican, mythical themes of satyrs, sphinxes, nymphs and harpies mix with the more orthodox symbolism of God as grey-bearded patriarch dividing the waters from the land in the moment of creation.

Even when Biblical themes ceased to dominate European art, symbolism continued to play an important role because of its close links with creativity itself. Both symbolism and creativity stem from unconscious processes, and some of the symbolic themes in visual art are not apparent to the artists themselves until they later analyse their work.

Perseus and Andromeda
This painting by the 17th-century Dutch artist Joachim Utewael is executed in the exaggerated, vividly coloured style of the Mannerist school. It shows the Greek hero Perseus rescuing Andromeda (the daughter of the king of Ethiopia) from the clutches of a sea monster sent by Poseidon (the god of the sea) to terrorize the land of Ethiopia. Perseus, shown flying above the sea monster with sword raised, is an animus figure (see page 13). The shells in the foreground symbolize not only journeys by sea, but also the feminine principle and sexual passion.

Hindu Gods in Art

Hindu deities may be readily identified by their distinctive attributes. Kali, the terrifying aspect of Devi (the great goddess), whose task it is to destroy demons who threaten the cosmic order, is depicted as black-faced hag wearing a necklace of skulls or heads. She is smeared with blood and wears a girdle of severed hands: in her four arms she holds a sword, noose, shield or cut-off head. In this painting Kali sits astride her consort, Shiva, one of the main Hindu deities. Shiva is typically represented as a white-skinned man (or hermaphrodite). He has a third eye (symbolizing his inner wisdom) and a crescent moon on his forehead. Brahma, the creator god (to the right of the picture), is usually shown with four faces. The origin of his appearance is described in myth: Brahma produced a beautiful woman from his own body and was smitten by her beauty. As she walked around him as a gesture of respect, Brahma's wish to stare at her beauty caused a succession of faces to appear.

The Search for Inner Wisdom

Patients in Jungian analysis are encouraged to identify and focus upon symbols that hold special meaning for them. At first these symbols may appear spontaneously in their dreams and doodles, but over time they become personalized, take on deeper levels of meaning, and come to represent aspects of the psyche that had previously remained unexpressed or difficult to put into words. By revealing pathways into the psyche, symbols can help the patient to reconcile the demands of the conscious and unconscious minds, and thereby bring about psychological health and stability. This use of symbols is not the exclusive province of modern psychiatry. All the major religious traditions have, through meditation, harnessed the power of symbols in the quest for inner peace and spiritual wisdom.

The essential element in the technique of meditation is to prevent the mind from becoming lost in random thoughts by focusing upon a single symbol (which may be auditory, visual or tactile) without trying rationally to reflect on its meaning. The symbol stimulates thoughts and insights, which are simply observed and allowed to pass out of awareness. The aim of meditation is to move beyond linguistic interpretations (though these may have their value when thought about consciously afterwards) and uncover a level of intuitive understanding beyond language, which profoundly changes the way we experience the world and ourselves.

In theory, anything from a meaningless scribble to an itch on the nose can act as a focus for meditation, but in practice most meditative traditions use archetypal symbols as their points of departure, because they provide a surer pathway back into the collective unconscious from which they originally emerged. In native North American and other shamanic traditions, nature herself provides these symbols, so the meditator might gaze upon distant mountains, listen to the sound of the wind, or concentrate upon the feel of the earth under his or her seated body. The Cathars – a 13th-century heretical Christian sect – meditated upon the reflection of a candle flame in water, and the flame is still used as a focus in certain forms of yoga. In the Tibetan practice of *tumo*, the adept concentrates upon increasing the feeling of heat in the depths of the belly, and circulating it through the chakras (see page 182) and from there through the rest of the body. In certain forms of Hindu and Buddhist meditation, a deity or the Buddha is visualized in meticulous detail, replete with symbolic colours and adornments, and then pictured descending through the crown of the meditator's head and coming to rest in the heart.

Symbols and Meditation
To use an archetypal symbol, such as the rosy cross, as a focus for meditation, gaze at it, blinking only when your eyes start to burn. Try to avoid judging any thoughts that arise while focusing on the symbol, and allow it to enter your consciousness as if it is communicating with a rosy cross that is already there. As the meditation progresses and your inner image of the cross becomes clearer, close your eyes and feel yourself going deeper and deeper into your visualization, as if you are going on a journey into yourself. With time and patience, the image will begin to release a rush of intuitive ideas.

By holding the image in your mind on the verge of sleep it can be persuaded to appear in your dreams, where its inner significance will be revealed through its relationships with aspects of the unconscious (see pages 46–49).

The Tibetan Bardomandala

In certain advanced forms of Buddhist meditation on a mandala (see page 60), each section of the geometrical design symbolizes a different meaning, which is usually referred to as a "deity". These symbolizations are not arbitrarily imposed upon the designs, but represent insights that emerged originally in the minds of spiritual masters. These deities can be regarded as personifications of the energies (emotional and physical) that go to make up life; but, like all true symbols, they are "real" in that they represent a profound reality beyond mere figments of the meditator's imagination.

Dream Symbols

Interpreting Dream Symbolism
A dream is a narrative, and often a highly condensed one, spanning an awesome amount of material by means of its own specialized symbolic shorthand. Although many dream symbols are associated with universal archetypes, their precise meanings are mutable, depending on the psychology of the dreamer and on the context in which they appear in the dream. For this reason the so-called dream dictionaries, which claim to give objective interpretations of every dream scenario, are of limited value.

In order to understand dream language, we need first to study the meanings attached by various cultures to the most commonly occurring symbols. The World of Symbols directory in this book (pages 50–139) is a good place to start. Next, we need to record the symbols that present themselves in our dreams and identify those features within the dream – people, objects, colours, or animals – that have the greatest impact upon us. We need also to note the emotions which these features arouse in us, and the events within which they occur. Many symbols are ambivalent, and can present themselves in our dreams in either positive or negative roles. Our emotional response to them is a good indication of which of these roles they play. By keeping a dream diary, we can identify recurring symbols and look for patterns in our dreams, which is of greater value than asking ourselves the meaning of an isolated dream. The dream diary allows us to analyse consciously the insights gained during dreams in the context of our social and psychological lives, and to move toward an integrated understanding of the relevance of our dream symbols.

Dreams are involuntary products of the psyche. They present us with a bewildering array of images and feelings, familiar and unfamiliar, all of which have something to teach us. The communicative power of dreams has been acknowledged for millennia: the ancients credited them with the power of prophecy, and in Egypt the gods were believed to speak through the dreams of the Pharoahs. However, the interpretation of dreams has always been fraught with uncertainty, because the messages they carry often emerge in an ambiguous and indistinct symbolic form.

Some dreams function at the *non-symbolic level* (level 1) and can be taken at face value, representing in an easily identifiable form the experiences and preoccupations of the past day or days – material arising mostly from the preconscious (see page 11). Dreams that function at the *mundane symbolic level* (level 2) go much deeper, using symbols to express material that originates primarily in the personal unconscious (see page 11). Such dreams relate to basic physical preoccupations, such as food, bodily comfort and health, emotions and self-sympathy (the so-called self-preservation needs), as well as sexual preoccupations, such as sensuality, orgasm and sexual dominance or submission (the so-called species preservation needs). Although these themes could be explored linguistically in a dream, they are frequently so exciting and alarming that if confronted directly by the mind, the result would be instant arousal from sleep. By disguising as symbols and metaphors the material it is presenting, the dream may be, as Freud put it, the "guardian of sleep", enabling us to enjoy the physical and psychological benefits that sleep brings. Level 2 dreams are often confusing in both content and presentation, reflecting the muddle that constitutes much of our psychological life.

Dreams that operate at the *higher symbolic level* (level 3) touch on our desire to find a meaning in life beyond the physical, emotional and sexual, and stem primarily from the collective unconscious (see page 11). Jung referred to them as "great dreams", because they carry a powerful, usually uplifting, emotional charge, and remain clear in the mind of the dreamer for many years. In most cases these dreams contain archetypal images, which are part of the universal symbolic language that anthropologists and psychologists have identified running right across cultures. Typically, they are clearly presented and "stage-managed", as if some director had resolved that we should leave the dream theatre with no confusion in our minds. Level 3 dreams are thought to operate symbolically because they are associated with a part of the unconscious that evolved before mankind acquired speech, and

Dream Logic

In some dreams, symbols crowd in upon each other and appear impossibly confused. Such dreams may actually contain several interwoven narratives: their meanings eventually emerge if we look keenly enough for them. Absurd, illogical and dream-like juxtapositions featured in the work of the Surrealists, such as Belgian artist René Magritte, whose painting *Le Jouer Secret* is shown above.

Content and Context

Dream symbols should always be related to the context in which they occur. For example, a parasol, which is a universally positive symbol, may indicate the loss of protection or status if the dream shows it being blown away in the wind. Conversely, a skeleton, normally a rather grim symbol, may represent the end of an anxiety or of an unhappy relationship.

which therefore functions pre-linguistically. They contain psychological material that cannot be put into words; and although the archetypal images they contain may speak during the dream, their words are associated more with those areas of consciousness which remain active during sleep than with anything directly expressed by the symbols themselves. It is as if the meaning contained in the symbols is recognized and to some degree translated into words by the mind, even during sleep.

Dreams have a quirky, idiosyncratic way of handling their material. In dreams, symbols often undergo sudden, puzzling transformations. We leap onto the back of a horse only to find it has changed into a hammock swinging under a tree. We enter a cave only to discover ourselves in the nave of a great cathedral. We open a book that transforms itself into a chess board complete with chess men. And so on. Yet these apparently bizarre transformations are accepted without question by the dreaming mind. Either our critical faculties are left behind at the gates of sleep, or we recognize at the time that these transformations make their own kind of sense.

If they do, what kind of sense might this be? The answer is that symbols and dream events are connected together by meaning rather than by appearance. Thus, the horse changing into a hammock under a tree may indicate that by training an aspect of our powerful, instinctive nature (the horse) we may make life not only easier for ourselves (the hammock) but also more creative (the tree). The position of the hammock, mid-way between the roots and the branches of the tree, may also suggest a desirable balance between our animalistic side (the earth) and our spiritual side (the crown of the tree). Similarly, the cave changing into the nave of a cathedral may represent the need to go more deeply into the unconscious self (the cave) in order to find not only the space for which we may be longing in life (the vastness of the nave) but also the spiritual direction and guidance (the cathedral itself). And the book changing into a chess board may show that we need to put our theoretical wisdom (the book) into practice (the chess board).

We may dream of a train waiting at a crossing which suddenly becomes an elephant charging towards us, and of a gun which we draw to defend ourselves only to see it turn into an empty bottle. This dream seems to be offering us a new opening in our life (the waiting train) provided that we are prepared to change course (the crossing, at which road meets rail). At this point, anxiety enters the dream. The charging elephant (a symbol of higher authority) threatens to crush us unless we defend ourselves. However, our

Night Terrors
However frightening or irritating dream material may appear to be, it is worth remembering that it is trying to be helpful. Dreams draw our attention to aspects of our psychological life that we are in some way misusing or overlooking while awake. They stimulate, warn, motivate or remind us with images that carry sufficient emotional charge to alert us to their importance. Dream images clearly inspired the 18th-century Swiss artist, Henry Fuseli, in this painting entitled *The Nightmare*.

weapon (the gun), turns out to be useless (the transformation into the empty bottle). These examples show the clarity with which the dream narrative can be allowed to emerge, provided that we are prepared to spend time consciously analysing our dream symbols. And just as experience improves our proficiency at spoken languages, so it allows us to become more and more familiar with dream language, and with the way in which, through this language, our unconscious psychological life allows its hopes, warnings and fears to emerge into conscious awareness.

The World of Symbols

Symbols have been subjected to analysis by historians, archaeologists, ethnographers and psychologists. To date, however, no unified theory has emerged to account for the language of symbolism in the same way that grammatical theory explains the fundamental framework of spoken and written language. Symbols, unlike written words, are not limited by practical concerns: their abundance and variety is constrained only by the limits of the human imagination. They appear in every conceivable form – in pictures, metaphors, sounds, gestures, odours, myths and personifications – and draw on all sources, material and non-material, for their inspiration.

Jung argued that symbols constitute a universal idiom. Abstract shapes, which arise directly from the unconscious without any allusion to the natural world, are indeed encountered worldwide. The "Christian" symbol of the cross was used by the Assyrians to represent the sky god, Anu, and by the Chinese as a symbol of the earth. When the Spaniards, led by Hernán Cortés, landed in Mexico in 1519, they found in the native temples numerous depictions of the cross – the Toltec symbol of the gods Tlaloc and Quetzalcoatl. The invaders, however, did not consider that the cross could be anything other than a Christian symbol, and concluded that it had been carried to the Toltecs on a mission conducted by Saint Thomas, the legendary apostle of all the Indies. This story underlines the point that although symbols are a characteristic feature of humanity in general, they are also subject to widespread differentiation across cultural divides. Cultures and religions are largely defined by the symbols they use and venerate, and initiation into a particular symbol system helps to shape an individual's identity. By denying that the cross could be a Toltec symbol, the Spaniards were in effect protecting the integrity of their own religious beliefs.

But symbols are more than just historical and cultural signposts. They can help us toward a fuller understanding of our own minds. The entries on the following pages explore the meanings, esoteric and exoteric, of symbols: representing a sample of the huge array of symbolic forms, they provide an entry into this fascinating world.

Shapes and Colours

Shapes and colours are the building-blocks of all visual symbols, but are also deeply significant in their own right. Religions such as Judaism and Islam, which forbid the direct depiction of God's person, have developed an array of abstract shapes to represent aspects of divine energy. However, symbolic shapes also occur frequently in the cultures of ancient Egypt and Greece, and in those of Northern Europe, where naturalistic religious art is highly developed, and abstract symbols, such as quadrangles, circles and rows of dots, were a common theme in art as early as the Paleolithic Period (see pages 22–25).

The ubiquity of symbolic shapes stems partly from the fact that they are easily reproduced and recognized, but also suggests that they carry levels of meaning not easily conveyed through representational images. Over the years, the simplest forms were embellished and elaborated, taking on new strands of meaning. The Anglican Church, for example, today recognizes as authentic at least fifty variants of the Christian cross.

The use of colour in modern psychiatry to treat mental disorders reflects the belief that colour can influence the psyche directly and profoundly. The symbolic language of colour is most easily decoded in relation to the hues of the natural world. For example, the Chinese Han Emperors (206BC–AD200) chose the colour of their ritual robes according to the particular aspect of nature to which their prayers were addressed. They wore white when petitioning the moon and red when appealing to the sun. Similarly, pink was seen by the Chinese as a symbol of approaching success because of its association with the colour of sunrise.

Shapes can be combined to generate new levels of meaning. For example, upward- and downward-pointing triangles (symbols of male and female energies respectively) form the diablo – a symbol of sexual union – when placed point to point. Similarly, colour combinations have specific connotations: for example, when paired with white, red represents mortality, because the shedding of blood leads to the pallor of death.

Rainbow Colours
In Christian tradition, the seven colours of the rainbow symbolize the seven gifts of the Holy Spirit to the Church – the sacraments, doctrine, office, polity, prayer and the powers to loosen and to bind.

Concentric Circles

A series of circles, one inside the other, is widely found as a symbol of the cosmos. This symbolic map of the universe from the 16th-century text *The Fine Flower of* *Histories* shows the sun, with its seven spheres, at the heart of the world. The map combines astrology with the science of letters, and was used in divination.

Sacred Geometry

Certain geometrical shapes have the power to reach deep into the unconscious and effect subtle changes in the mood of the observer. This property is perhaps most apparent when applied by a skilful architect. For example, visitors to classic Greek sites such as the Parthenon often experience a sense of inner tranquillity that can linger for days or even weeks. Similarly, the soaring grandeur of Europe's Gothic cathedrals resonates with some deep-seated potentiality within the observer, and evokes a sense of boundless spiritual possibilities.

The most direct explanation for the psychological power of abstract shapes is that they symbolize certain human emotions. An abrupt shape with irregular, jagged edges for most people symbolizes anger or anxiety, while a symmetrical, rounded shape represents feelings of relaxation and inner peace. It is possible that the near-universal meanings of certain shapes reflect some pattern-making ability within the mind itself. There is firm evidence that some geometric forms are innately more pleasing than others: certainly babies are more strongly attracted to symmetrical, harmonious shapes than to unbalanced, uneven ones.

This preference may have as its source the symmetry of the human face, and the feelings of well-being and comfort associated with the parental face from an early age. Moreover, when a child looks at inanimate objects and begins to experience its own movements, it is profoundly aware of a sense of balance, and this awareness may with time become translated into visual terms. Our feelings about geometry may also be concerned with the intrinsic balance within nature itself, each state of mind counterweighted and in part defined by its opposite. This theme of balance is particularly evident in the symbolic meanings of the cross, perhaps the most widespread and ancient of all symbols. In many cultures it represents the cosmos: the vertical line stands for the spiritual, masculine principle, and the horizontal for the earthly, feminine principle. The intersection is the point at which heaven and earth meet, and the result of their union is mankind – symbolized by the cross itself.

The Circle
Early in history the circle became a symbol of male divinity, appearing later as the haloes around the heads of angels. Lacking beginning or end, it represents infinity, perfection and the eternal. It is often used as a symbol of God.

The Square
This form represents solidity: a perfection that is static, earthly and material. It connotes dependability, honesty, shelter, safety. As the most frequent shape in Hindu symbology, it stands for order in the universe and the balance of opposites.

The Triangle
The magical number three represents the sacred Trinity. Pointing upward, the triangle stands for ascent to heaven, fire, the active male principle: reversed, it symbolizes grace descending from heaven, water, the passive feminine element.

The Three Realms
In this 17th-century design the basic shapes of circle, square (or rectangle) and triangle are used to represent the realms of God, mankind and Satan. The upper circle (1) is Jehovah, the infinite first cause, with the triangular rays of creation streaming both outward and inward; the lower circle (2) represents the world of angels and higher spiritual elements operating under God. The four triangles represent heaven (3), denoted by stars, angels and the symbol of the planet Mercury, rising above the

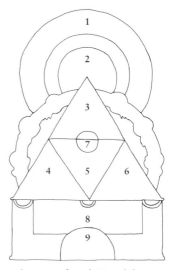

elements of earth (4; sulphur, stones and beasts), air (5; meteors, planets and birds), and water (6; metals, fish and salt). Mankind is symbolized by the circle (7) straddling heaven and earth. The rectangle (8) at the base stands for the realms of hell and within them fire and chaos. Satan is the semicircle (9), a symbol of incompleteness.

The Crescent
Just as the crescent moon changes into the full moon and back again, the crescent symbolizes change within the world of forms. It represents the newborn, and also the magical power that can transform shape. Because the crescent moon rides across the night sky, it has also come to symbolize the ship of light that carries the soul through the darkness and into the light of the new dawn. The crescent is an emblem of Islam. When paired with a star, it represents sovereignty and divinity.

The Buddhist Wheel of Life
One of the symbolic meanings of the circle is the constant cycle of change, and this is graphically demonstrated in the Buddhist wheel of life. At the top of the wheel are the heavenly realms, followed (clockwise) by the realms of the titans (jealous gods), the hungry ghosts (earth-bound spirits), the animals, and mankind. Holding the wheel is Yama, lord of death, who devours all. In the centre are symbols of the three delusions that keep humans on the wheel of life and out of Nirvana – a red cock (lust), a green snake (hatred) and a black pig (ignorance).

The Celtic Cross
The Celtic cross, which brings together the cross and the circle, pre-dates Christianity by many centuries. Its original symbolism was associated with fertility, the cross standing for the male generative power and the circle for the female. Within Christianity it represents the union of heaven and earth.

The Oval
A symbol of the female genitalia, and thus of the female principle itself. When horizontal it becomes the all-seeing eye, best known in the form of the eye of Horus (the Egyptian lord of the skies). It appears in pagan cultures as a symbol for the sun god and in Christian iconography represents God the Father.

The Inverted Cross
In legend, Saint Peter was crucified upside-down, feeling himself unworthy to be crucified on the upright cross of Christ. The inverted cross therefore came to represent humility. It also shares the symbolism of the inverted tree of life – the idea that spirituality has its roots in heaven and reaches downward toward the earth.

The Ankh
Prominent in the symbolism of ancient Egypt, the ankh carries some of the meanings of the Celtic cross, and the idea of a key to unlock the mysteries of heaven and earth. Combining the symbols of Osiris (the *tau* or T cross) and Isis (the oval), it is a symbol of immortality, and is often depicted as being carried by the gods.

The Swastika
This widespread symbol is particularly revered by the Jains, the Buddhists and followers of Vishnu. It is essentially a cross spinning at its centre, with the angles at the end of each arm representing light streaming as the cross turns. Spinning clockwise, it symbolizes male energy; anticlockwise, female. In Jainism, the four arms represent the four levels of existence. The anticlockwise form has been debased into a symbol of black magic and negative energies.

The Rosy Cross
This symbol echoes the Celtic cross, and its early meanings are also linked with generative power. Its more esoteric use by the Rosicrucians suggested the blood of Christ spilled on the cross and the seven stages of initiation, represented by the seven rows of seven petals that form the flower.

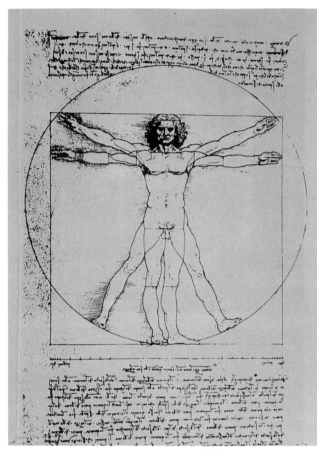

Universal Man
The shape of the human body carries great symbolic significance.
Even the gods are mostly shown in human form, and the Bible tells
us that God made Man "in His own image". Man's body is held to
be a reflection of the structure of the universe, displaying all its
components and characteristics.

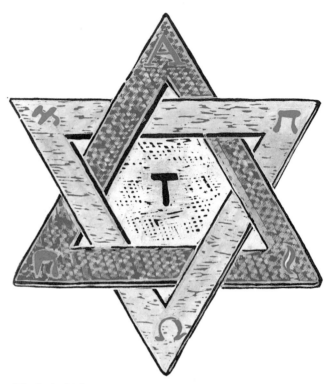

The Seal of Solomon
Of great antiquity, the Seal of Solomon appears in the writings and
practices of magicians, and has strong associations with Hebrew
mysticism: hence its appearance as the Star of David. The upward-
pointing triangle of fire and masculine energy meets the downward-
pointing triangle of water and the feminine, the two merging in
perfect harmony. The base of each triangle bisects the other just
under the apex, forming the symbols for air and earth. The Seal
therefore portrays the four elements, which are combined with the
number three (the triangle) to produce the magical number seven.
However, as the Seal only has six points, the seventh is said to
invisible, representing the spiritual element of transformation,
which emerges to the inner eye of the magician as he meditates
upon the Seal.

The Eye as Geometry
In addition to the symbolism of its oval shape (see page 57), the eye
carries other kinds of geometrical significance. This illustration,
from an 18th-century Arab manuscript, shows the eye as an oval
containing two circles, the inner of which encloses a mandala of
divine wisdom. The eye takes the outside world into the inner, and
can also project the inner world onto the outer. Certain mythical
beings, such as Medusa (see page 82), had the power to transmit
their intentions through their gaze – the so-called evil eye.

The Celtic Triple Enclosure
This ancient Celtic symbol represents human consciousness. The outer square is that part of the mind that relates to the physical world through the senses. The inner square is the unconscious mind through which come visions of the gods and other worlds. The middle square is the part of the mind receptive to both physical world and spirit.

The Pentagram
Being endless, like the circle, the pentagram, or pentacle, stands for perfection and wholeness. At the same time its triangular components stand for the four elements plus spirituality. These twin properties give the symbol power to bind or banish evil spirits, and make it a favourite of magicians.

The Stupa
Originally built to house relics of the Buddha or his disciples, the stupa came to be used as an all-embracing symbol. The square base represents earth, the circle water, the triangle fire, the semicircle air, and the flame ether. Energy flows upward through decreasingly dense levels of matter until it transforms into spirituality.

The Pyramid
The most evocative of three-dimensional symbols, the pyramid represents the world axis. Its apex symbolizes the highest point of spiritual attainment, with the body of the structure representing man's ascent through the hierarchy of enlightenment. In the ancient world, the pyramids may have been the scenes of initiation into mystery cults, which took the initiate through the portals of death into the realms beyond, to return him to the world transformed.

Mandalas and Yantras

In mandalas and yantras, which reach their most intricate and evocative form in the iconography of India and Tibet, the symbolism of geometrical shapes is used to maximum effect. Not only are these diagrams sacred works of art, they also act as a focus for deep meditation. Each of these complex forms is essentially a depiction of the universe and of the forces and gods that drive it. By meditating on the symbol, and moving mentally toward its centre, the seeker is made aware of deep levels of meaning.

The shapes that appear most frequently in mandalas and yantras are circles, squares and triangles. Combinations of these forms can produce extraordinary visual effects, conveying the idea that nothing exists except as an encounter between various fields of energy, just as a rainbow is created only when sunlight, water and the visual activity of the observer come together. Through meditation on the yantra, the mind is gradually able to "unscramble" the sets of relationships which give an illusory sense of permanence to the outside world.

There are no rigid differences between mandalas and yantras, but the former usually contain lettering or the human form (in the shape of Buddhas, bodhisattvas and attendant deities), while the latter are primarily geometrical, with the human form, if it appears at all, taking on a more peripheral function. Yantras provide a more advanced focus for meditation because they represent the realities that lie beyond the world of physical forms. Psychologists have noted that mandala-like shapes are drawn spontaneously in psychotherapy by people with no grounding in Eastern mysticism: such drawings are thought to represent an attempt by the conscious self to recognize and integrate unconscious knowledge.

Om Mani Padme Hum ("Hail to the jewel in the lotus")
The ovoid shapes in the outer circle represent the petals of a lotus: around them are the Tibetan symbols for the mantra *Om Mani Padme Hum*. In the inner circle is the symbol for enlightenment. Shape and lettering combine to help the meditator focus on the opening of the "inner lotus" to reveal the jewel within the self.

The Sri Yantra
The Sri Yantra is a powerful aid to meditation. Increasing in complexity from the centre outward, the pattern helps the observer to look symbolically back to the moment of creation, both of the universe itself, and of the acts through which the mind ceaselessly brings the outer world into existence.

Avalokiteshvara

In this Nepalese mandala, the bodhisattva of compassion, Avalokiteshvara, is shown in his eight-armed form, each arm holding a symbol of his concern for humanity. A bodhisattva is an enlightened being who refuses to enter Nirvana until all other sentient beings are saved. Avalokiteshvara symbolizes the compassionate side of our own nature, which we can awake by meditating on his mandala. His spirit is believed to be reborn in the Dalai Lama, the spiritual and temporal leader of Tibet.

Mazes and Labyrinths

The maze or labyrinth exercises a universal fascination for mankind. It appears in the symbolism of the ancient Egyptians and all the early Mediterranean civilizations. It was depicted by the Celtic peoples in pre-Christian times and also in Indian and Tibetan cultures before appearing as a motif in medieval Christianity. The symbolic meaning of the maze in many of these cultures reflects the idea of an inner journey through the confusing and conflicting pathways of the mind until the seeker reaches the centre and discovers the essential reality of his or her own nature.

Mazes can be formed from hedges, banks, walls or any convenient barriers, or they can simply be traced out on the ground or painted on a ceiling. Not all are puzzles: so-called unicursal labyrinths have a single route serpentining around itself until it arrives at the centre, so that there is no fear of losing the way. In early European civilizations, such labyrinths were often the scenes of ritual dances, with all members of a community holding hands and following one another through the pathway into the hub: this exercise was of great value in increasing social cohesion through shared experience. In contrast, passing through a multicursal maze – one in which the path divides repeatedly and there is a risk of becoming disoriented – is a much more individual and potentially threatening exercise. It symbolizes the way in which the mind can easily become confused and sidetracked in its attempts to find the way back to the source of its own being.

For the ancient Egyptians the maze may have symbolized the path through the underworld followed by the dead, with Isis as guide and Osiris standing in judgment at the centre. In an abstraction of this idea, the maze came to represent the mysterious, feminine, creative power that served as both bringer of life and, in the role of queen of darkness and of night, bringer of the sleep of death.

The Way of Truth
Christianity first saw the maze as a symbol of the path of ignorance leading away from God, but by the 14th century it had recovered its positive symbolism and denoted the true way of belief. It was widely used in architecture, for example, on the floor of Chartres Cathedral (above) and on a ceiling in the Ducal Palace, Mantua (right).

The Clock Maze
With no escape from its tyranny and no resting place until the centre (eternal life) is reached, the labyrinth is an apt symbol for time itself. Human life is bounded by time and whichever way we turn, we find no destination other than the centre, a symbol of mystic return to the womb.

The Labyrinth and the Minotaur

The multicursal maze is exemplified by the labyrinth of Crete in which Theseus tracked down and killed the Minotaur. Theseus represents the traveller guided by divine instinct (a golden thread) through the labyrinth of life and overcoming the debased, animalistic side of his own nature.

Pathways

Mazes appear frequently in dreams, often in the form of confusing pathways through a forest or a strange town, before which the dreamer hesitates in fear and perplexity. Here the symbolism is that of confusion or indecision in the dreamer's life when he or she is faced by many choices, the outcome of each of which is thought to be uncertain.

Numbers and Sounds

Numbers are far more than a convenient measure of the physical world. In many traditions they are considered to be the primal organizing principle that gives structure to the universe. The lives of animals and plants, the seasons and the movements of the planets are all governed by numerical relationships; and the shapes of crystals and harmony in music are determined by numerical laws. Numbers are seen as universal templates of creation, and therefore as symbols of perfection and of the gods. In the Greek and Hebrew alphabets, a number was assigned to each letter, and great importance was attached to the numerical significance of a name or phrase: the idea that all things can be expressed in terms of numbers persists today in the divinatory pseudo-science of numerology.

Sound is an evocative and thus a creative experience. Many cultures credit the gods with the power to make sounds, either through natural agencies, such as wind, water and animals, or through musical instruments. In myth, sound can be bewitching (the voices of the sirens), or destructive (the shout with which Joshua and the Israelites felled the walls of Jericho). Many creation myths talk of sound disturbing the pre-existent stillness, thereby bringing the world into being.

Three
The number three underlies all aspects of creation – mind, body and spirit; birth, life and death; past, present and future. The trinity occurs in many religions, symbolizing unity in diversity. The three magi (above) symbolize Christ's divinity, majesty and sacrifice.

Four
The number of mankind (the four-limbed), four is associated with wholeness and completion – four elements, cardinal points, seasons, and ages of man. To the Chinese, it was the number of the earth.

Seven
The sum of the number of divinity (three) and the number of mankind (four), seven represents the macrocosm and the microcosm, and expresses the relationship between God and humanity. Accordingly, the world was created in seven days, there are seven deadly sins that separate mankind from God, and seven stages of initiation (seven heavens) through which we have to journey in order to return to God. The number was sacred to the Greek god Apollo and Ishtar, the Babylonian goddess of fertility.

Nine
The divine number three multiplied by itself gives nine, the incorruptible number of completion and eternity. Nine is associated with the circle, the square and the triangle. For the Chinese, it was the celestial number, the most auspicious of all, and there were nine great social laws and nine classes of officials. In Hinduism, nine squared produces the 81-square mandala, which symbolizes the universe and is used as an aid in prophecy and in astrological calculations.

M
The letter "M" indicates the union between man and woman, who are shown sheltering under its arches.

Om
The sound "Om" (pronounced ar-oo-mm) is believed by Hindus to be the sound that brought creation into being.

The Mantra
In Hinduism and Buddhism the mantra is a sacred sound, which symbolically expresses a particular divine energy. Mantras can be spoken aloud or just sounded in the mind. Initiation into certain sects involves the guru whispering the mantra into the ear of the initiate.

Colours

Colour is one of the areas in daily life in which symbolism is most readily apparent. This is because colours have an immediate impact on our emotions, possessing the power to arouse or to tranquillize, to gladden or to depress. Psychologists suggest that the effects of colours on the mind derive from their associations with the natural world (blue sky, red blood, gold sun and so on), while occultists put forward more esoteric explanations, linking the seven colours of the spectrum with the magical number seven and with the number of notes on the musical scale. At a deeper level, colour symbolizes an essential creative quality within life itself, so that death is seen as either black or white, both of which are the absence of observable colour.

Colour symbolism may affect even the use of colour for obviously practical purposes. For example, heraldry is thought by some to have incorporated the Kabbalists' interpretation of black as the colour of wisdom.

Red
Symbolizing the life-force as expressed through the animal world, red is the energy coursing through the body, the colour that flushes the face and swims before the eyes in violent emotional arousal. Red is the colour of war and its god, Mars, and of the greatest of the Roman gods, Jupiter (left). It is the colour of masculinity and activity. To the Chinese, red represents good luck; to the Christian, it denotes Christ's passion.

Gold
The colour of the sun, gold is the symbol of majesty and of the divine principle expressed through matter. For the Egyptians, it was linked with Ra, the sun god, and corn, upon which life depended. To the Hindu it was the symbol of truth. The ancient Greeks saw gold as the symbol of reason and immortality – the latter represented in myth by the golden fleece (right), which was found by Jason hanging on the tree of life.

Blue
Blue is the hue of intellect, peace and contemplation. It represents water and coolness, and symbolizes the sky, infinity, the emptiness from which existence arises and to which it returns. To the Christian, blue is the colour of the Virgin as Queen of Heaven (right), and denotes faith, compassion and the waters of baptism. The ancient Greeks and Romans attributed the colour blue to Venus, the goddess of love.

Green

Symbolizing the life of the sensations, green also stands for nature – not only growth but also decay. Linked also with jealousy, it is an ambivalent colour. A positive link is with *Tir Nan Og,* the Celtic isle of the blessed (above), to which the soul migrated through the fog of death.

Black

In the West, black is the symbol of death, sorrow and the underworld. The black cat (above) seen as a portent of good luck is a relatively modern notion. To the Hindus black represents time, and Kali, the destroying goddess. To the Egyptians it was the colour of rebirth and resurrection.

White

White represents purity, virginity and the transcendent, yet it also suggests the pallor of death, and in the Orient is the colour of mourning. For the Tibetans, white is the colour of Mount Meru, the mountain "at the centre of the world" (above), embodying ascent to enlightenment.

Violet

Combining the power and authority of red with the sanctity and wisdom of blue, violet is the most mystical of colours. As a focus for meditation it can raise consciousness to higher levels. Violet also denotes sorrow and mourning. It is worn here (right) by the nymph Echo, who pined for the love of Narcissus.

Yellow

While hinting at some of the qualities of gold, yellow also suggests faithlessness and betrayal. A yellow flag was used in the West to symbolize disease and quarantine. But in China this was the national colour, sacred to the Emperor (right). To the Buddhist, yellow is the colour of humility, hence its use in the monk's saffron robe.

Objects

As fragments of the physical world, objects are often imbued with special significance because they span the divide between the inexpressible inner reality that each individual builds up from instinct, intuition and experience, and the outer world of forms. The deepest symbolic meanings are held by objects that resonate with the preoccupations of people everywhere at all times – food, sex, conflict and the gods.

The earliest known sculptures, the Venus statuettes of the Paleolithic Period (see page 25), were probably fertility charms. By handling these amulets (many are polished and worn from touching) the ancients silently petitioned the spirits believed to rule over birth and regeneration. Such talismans appear in nearly all cultures, and in the West they still survive, albeit in a debased form, as lucky charms. Talismans are usually representations of a god or goddess: they serve as constant reminders to the deity of the supplicant's existence, but are also embodiments of the god's powers and are themselves capable of influencing events. Other objects are of spiritual significance because they help to focus prayer and meditation. The spinning of a Buddhist prayer wheel is a way of offering up the prayer or mantra inscribed upon it. Similarly, the beads of the Christian rosary and the *mala* carried by Moslems present the devotee with a structure for his or her prayers. The beads carry the symbolism of the circle (see page 54) and also have numerical significance. For example, ninety-nine beads on the Islamic *mala* stand for the Divine names: the hundredth bead is silent and represents the name that can only be known in Paradise.

When fashioning an object from wood, stone or metal, the craftsman is cast in the role of creator. In the belief that the artefact contains the creator's energy, craftsmen of past civilizations often engaged in meditation and purification rituals before starting work. This practice is still alive in modern Japan among the blacksmiths who make ceremonial weapons.

The Hourglass
A symbol of mortality and the passing of time, the hourglass also stands for the cyclical nature of existence (because hourglasses have to be inverted repeatedly), and for the grace of the heavens falling upon the earth.

The Grail and the Round Table
In medieval Christian tradition, the circular table represents
the universe, totality and perfection. The Holy Grail (the
legendary chalice used by Christ at the Last Supper, and later
a receptacle for his blood) stands at the centre of this
wholeness, and is the key to salvation.

Royalty, Office and Consecration

Many of the trappings of office are highly symbolic, expressive variously of status, superior wisdom, access to secret powers, wealth and riches, or temporal or spiritual authority. Such attributes help to maintain the mystique of those who hold high position, and are constant reminders of the extent to which such people are set apart from lesser mortals.

A potent symbol of office is the key, a mark of initiation: it is an attribute of the pope, and of the two-faced Roman god Janus, who held the key that both binds mankind to the gods and frees us from the lower self. The shepherd's crook carried by Osiris and the Egyptian kings, and also metaphorically by Christ, denotes leadership and protection. The flail, another attribute of Osiris, symbolizes judgment: it survives to this day in the form of the flyswatter carried by African tribal chiefs.

The Baptismal Font
Baptism is a symbolic cleansing of sins – rebirth in the life-sustaining fluid of the earth-mother's womb. Fonts are therefore often eight-sided (the number of regeneration). Placed inside the west entrance to a church, they symbolize entry into the Christian way of life.

The Throne
As a powerful symbol of monarchy, wisdom and divinity, the throne can represent the relationship between God and mankind. In Buddhism and Orthodox Christianity the empty throne symbolizes the most high, whose features are too glorious to be portrayed.

The Crown
The symbolism of the crown has two components: its circularity represents perfection and the infinite, and its height indicates majesty. A gold crown stands for masculine, solar power, a silver crown for lunar, feminine power. The Virgin Mary (the queen of heaven) has a crown of stars.

The Coat of Arms
From its 12th-century origin as an aid to identification in battle, the coat of arms came to symbolize identity, office and honours conferred upon the bearer. The design of arms is subject to strict conventions: only certain colours and symbols (or charges) are permitted, and the status of the bearer – spinster, married man, first son and so on – is denoted by specific modifications. The shield is the oldest and most important component of the coat of arms: the crest and supporters (often animals) were 14th-century additions.

The Orb
Carried by a monarch at coronation, the orb represents temporal power: the surmounting cross embodies spiritual authority. The ceremonial orb and sceptre suggest dominion over female and male energies, which together symbolize the creative forces of the material world.

The Oil Lamp
In the Greco-Roman and later in the Christian world, anointment with oil was symbolic of consecration, dedication and wisdom.

The Fleur de Lys
Adopted as the royal emblem by the kings of France, the triple lily stands for the triple majesty of God, his creation, and royalty. The lily also represents the trinity of mind, body and soul, which come together only in mankind.

War and Peace

The importance of war and peace in human affairs is reflected in a rich symbolic vocabulary. War is conventionally portrayed as destruction and disturbance of equilibrium, as a violator of beauty or as a visitation of hell upon earth. Peace is seen as healing and fertility, the ravaged land returned to the plough and the weapons of war converted to constructive purposes. However, these depictions are by no means universal. For example, war may be presented as a crusade, a cleansing process or the victory of good over evil, and peace is sometimes represented as sloth, complacency, or the degeneration of youthful vigour. At a psychological level, war can suggest mental turmoil and the battle between the desires of the flesh and the dictates of the spirit. It also represents the destructive forces of madness and psychological fragmentation. Through its identification with aggressive energy, war can also symbolize masculinity (the gods of war in all cultures are predominantly male), and initiation into manhood. Peace can stand for maturity of mind, and the reconciliation of all opposites: associated with passive, receptive energy, it sometimes denotes femininity, the power that creates and nurtures life.

Weapons were often adorned with symbolic forms in the belief that their power would be enhanced. In Christianity, the hilt of the sword was shaped in the form of the cross, and battering rams sometimes had the head of a ram carved at the front. Similarly, the two heads of the battle-axe symbolized divine and material power. Arms and armies were frequently blessed before battle, and prior to being knighted, a squire would keep an all-night vigil before the church altar, his weapons and armour at his feet, so that by morning they would be sanctified to his use, and he to God.

The Dove and Olive Branch
A symbol of the end of the great flood, when the dove brought an olive branch to Noah. The dove is the classic representation of peace, standing for the Holy Spirit.

Mars, Roman God of War
Mars is pictured in a chariot, itself a symbol of battle. The month of March – when armies were mobilized after the winter – is named after him.

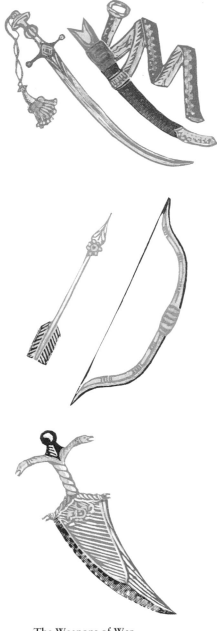

The Apocalypse
The Four Horsemen, perhaps the best-known representations of the apocalypse, have been variously depicted over the centuries. Dürer's 15th-century engraving *The Apocalypse* (above) shows War carrying a sword, the Conqueror holding a bow and accompanied by an angel, Famine, with a pair of scales, and Death holding a trident and riding a sickly, emaciated horse.

The Weapons of War
Like war itself, weapons can be positive symbols. The sword often stands for justice and authority; the bow and arrow for sunlight and for the pangs of love; the dagger for the phallus and masculinity in general.

Musical Instruments

Music and chanting evoke profound states of consciousness, and can actually stimulate mystical experiences. Music was likened to the primal sound that created the universe, and many occult traditions teach that the seven notes of the fundamental musical scale (and the seven colours of the spectrum) correspond to the seven rays that sustain existence. Music thus symbolized the order and harmony behind creation, and it seemed natural to make use of music to invoke the gods. In Hinduism, Lakshmi, consort of Vishnu, was believed to reside in musical instruments, and the enlightened soul itself was symbolized by the sounds the instruments produced.

The Lyre
Best known as a symbol of Orpheus, whose music charmed the birds from the trees, the lyre is also an attribute of Apollo, god of prophecy and music. It represents wisdom and moderation.

The Drum and Dance
Rhythm and dance are widely believed to imitate the process of divine creation and to bring men and women closer to their instinctive natures. Notable examples are the uninhibited dance of the Bacchantes (the devotees of Bacchus, god of wine) and the mannered Hindu temple dances, where each gesture is meticulously scripted. Death is also represented as a feverish dance, with people of all social rank compelled to join.

The Harp
Daghda, Celtic god of plenty, used a harp to summon the seasons. It also symbolizes passage to the next world.

The Horn
The sounding of the horn announces the end of the world or, in Jewish tradition, the approach of an enemy.

Knots, Cords and Rings

Symbolizing the binding together of people or objects, knots, cords and rings can have negative connotations of imprisonment and limitation, or positive ones of unity and initiation. For example, the sacred cord of the Hindu Brahmin stands for his link with Brahma, the absolute; however, Buddhism alludes to mortals "tied to" the wheel of becoming. Knots, like the labyrinth, can stand for the tortuous path to enlightenment, while the ring suggests protection, eternity and the absolute.

The Spiral
The ancients believed that energy, physical and spiritual, flowed in spiral form. The spiral represents both solar and lunar, masculine and feminine, energies.

The Plait
Representing the covenant between man and God, the plait featured in Christian art and architecture. This roof boss is from Southwark Cathedral, London.

The Endless Knot
In Celtic, Chinese and Hindu art, the endless knot represents the continuity, longevity and eternity. The design is often incorporated into bridal dresses and jewelry.

The Thread of Life
In Greek myth, the three Fates – Clotho, Lachesis and Atropos – respectively spin, measure and cut the thread of life, thus controlling a person's destiny from cradle to grave.

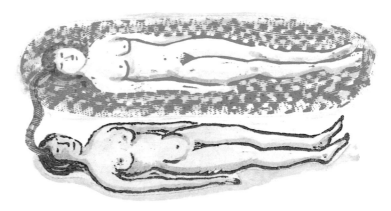

The Silken Cord
In occult traditions, the etheric body is said to be joined to the physical by means of a silken cord. In Greek myth, the precarious nature of existence is symbolized by the single hair that suspends a sword over the head of Damocles.

Buildings and Monuments

From Neolithic times, architecture has served mankind's emotional and spiritual as well as practical needs. Buildings therefore chronicle our developing thoughts about ourselves and the world, and reflect our higher aspirations. The dimensions of many structures, particularly sacred ones, have been strongly influenced by the symbolic meanings of form. Architects believed that by following certain geometric guidelines, their works would become infused by sacred power.

The traditional teachings of many religions propose the idea of the body as a temple of the spirit, created by the divine architect. Believing that the human form in some way mirrors the proportions of the macrocosm, earthly architects have used it as a template for their designs. Most Christian churches, for example, are laid out in the shape of the human body with arms outstretched. Similarly, many temples have an outer court, inner court and Holy of Holies, corresponding repectively to the abdomen (the organs of regeneration), the thorax (the organs of life and vitality) and the head (the organs of spiritual perception).

The Tomb
The ancients saw the tomb as a gateway to another life, and buried their dead with objects likely to be needed on the journey between the two worlds. In Europe, tombs of the rich were adorned with effigies symbolizing the earthly qualities (such as valour or fair-mindedness) of the deceased.

The Castle and Moat
The castle is used symbolically only in the West: it was important during the Crusades as a place of physical and spiritual refuge. It represents the stronghold of either good or evil, or a place in which treasure is guarded or a princess (often used as a symbol of enlightenment) is held captive.

The Door
This represents a barrier through which only initiates (those who have the key) can pass. It can also symbolize an opportunity, or transition to a new state of being, such as sleep or death. In Christian symbology, the three doors of a cathedral stand for faith, hope and charity.

The Bridge
A symbol of transition, particularly from life to death, or from the secular to the divine, the bridge can also represent danger on the path of psychological or spiritual development.

The Stone Circle (right)
The function of these great megalithic structures is still unclear. They may have been sites of worship, their circular structure symbolizing the cosmic eye of the Great Goddess, the universal mother. Some are known to have been astronomical markers, while others may have represented a link with the dead.

The Window
A symbol of the way in which our own consciousness looks out on and interprets the world. The window admits the light of God (to a church or temple), so it can also represent a person or thing acting as a vehicle for God.

The Temple
An obvious symbol of spiritual striving and attainment. Most temples were constructed to reflect the universe as a whole, as it was then perceived.

Animals

The ancient Egyptians believed that certain animals embodied the great creative forces (the gods) that form and sustain life. In having access to *all* these forces, mankind's position was higher than that of the animals, though this made us vulnerable to confusion and inner conflict. Only by looking to the animal world could humans learn how to develop or curb the creative forces within themselves to best effect.

Similar ideas occur in the shamanic traditions that once pervaded much of Asia, Europe and the Americas, and which still find living expression among the native North Americans and the peoples of Siberia and the Arctic. Animals were seen as a source of wisdom and power, not because they were greater than mankind, but because they were privy to the secrets of nature in a way that Man, hampered by his intellect, was not. Thus, animals could serve as guides to other worlds, as prophets, and as initiators into secret wisdom. To the shaman, the ability to communicate with animals, and the wearing of animal skins symbolized the restoration of the paradisal state.

In modern societies, certain animals are held to be omens of good or bad fortune, and some traditions maintain that humans should inform animals of important events such as births or marriages. The gods are represented as animals in Hindu and Buddhist art, and in Christian iconography, Christ and the four Evangelists appear in animal form (see page 41). However, it is now more usual for animals to symbolize the baser elements in human nature, such as lust, violence and greed, which must be tamed or killed. For example, Satan is often shown with the horns and tail of a goat, the nose of a vulture, the hooves of a horse and the wings of a bat; and in the Tibetan wheel of life (see page 56) the cock, the snake and the pig exemplify those baser human instincts that keep us tied to the realms of birth and death and prevent us from stepping off the wheel into Nirvana.

The Mouse
Sometimes representing humility, mice usually have negative symbolic meanings – hypocrisy in the Jewish tradition, destruction in the Christian (they may be shown gnawing at the Tree of Life).

The Dragonfly
A symbol of summer for the Chinese, the dragonfly was also held to represent instability because of its apparently haphazard flight. To the native American Indian it stood for swift activity.

The Butterfly
The butterfly is usually a positive symbol, standing for the powers of transformation and immortality, and for beauty arising out of apparent death and corruption (the seemingly lifeless cocoon).

Animal symbols
The profusion of animal symbolism in the mythology, art and
religion of all societies acknowledges the powerful influence of
instinct and emotions on human behaviour.

Dragons and Serpents

Dwelling in the dark caverns of the earth, with lungs of fire, wings of a bird and scales of a fish, the dragon epitomizes the four elements of the ancient world, unifying them into a single presence that can inspire the imagination and haunt our dreams. The dragon carries opposite meanings representing the paradox at the heart of our being – the mutual dependence of light and dark, creation and destruction, male and female. But more than any other symbol, the dragon also embodies the unifying force underlying these opposites. In itself it is neither good nor bad, but symbolizes the primal energy upholding the material world, which can be turned to either good or evil purposes.

In the Orient, the emphasis has traditionally been on the positive aspects of this primal energy. The dragon is depicted as a union of the beneficial powers of the elements. Uniting water (the serpent) with air (the bird, the breath of life), it represents the coming together of matter and spirit. This positive force was thought to be capable of animating the earth through the dragon pathways – symbolic arteries through which earth energy flows.

In pagan times the emphasis in the West, as in the East, was on the benificent aspects of dragon energy – as the Welsh flag, with its proud red dragon, still testifies. However, in the Christian era, with the relegation of the serpent to the symbolic role of Satan the tempter, the dragon came increasingly to represent chaos, raw destructive power, the evil inherent in the world of matter. Sometimes it is shown as coming between ourselves and hidden treasure (spiritual wisdom) or carrying off a virgin (purity) to its undergroud lair.

By an obvious logic, the dragon also came to symbolize the inner world of the emotions and the unconscious. In the West, it was the animal that lurks within us, the primitive energies which, left unbridled, can reduce us to the level of beasts.

The Dragonslayer
This image symbolizes the triumph of spirit over matter. The lance is a symbol of masculine power, and of the sun's rays slanting into the world.

Dragon Rising from the Sea
In the East, this was linked with scholarship and the creative mind. In the West, it was the symbol of the depths of the unconscious and the strange energies that dwell there.

The Chinese Imperial Dragon
The four claws of Mang, the terrestrial dragon, represent the four
elements. Lung, the imperial dragon (above), was blessed with a
fifth claw, representing ether – the spiritual power that was fully
mainfested in the person of the Emperor.

Ouroboros

The snake swallowing its own tail brings together the symbolism of the circle and of the serpent. It is the water-element equivalent of the phoenix, representing totality, rebirth, immortality, and the round of existence. It occurs in ancient Greece and Egypt.

Medusa

In Greek myth Medusa was once beautiful, but having made love in the temple of Athene, she was changed by the goddess into a harridan, with snakes for hair, who could turn a man into stone with her gaze. She symbolizes fear, specifically men's fear of women's swift transformations of mood. Medusa's head frequently appeared as a protective talisman on weapons and shields.

The Seven-headed Serpent

This symbol carries a double meaning. On one level it is Lotan, destroyed by Baal in the Canaanite myth, and probably the original Biblical Leviathan, which later served as a symbol of the seven deadly sins. On another level it is the combination of dragon or serpent with the mystical number seven, the number of the universe. As such, it represents the creative force in its most purposeful and complete form.

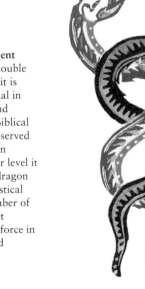

Entwined snakes

A symbol of the dual creative forces (good and evil) within the world of forms. When twined around a staff, the two snakes form the caduceus, symbol of the messenger of the gods, Hermes (Mercury to the Romans). In myth, the caduceus was formed when Hermes used the staff to separate two serpents locked in combat, and thus came to symbolize peace. It is used nowadays as a symbol for homeopathic medicine, reflecting the notion that nature can cure herself.

Heraldic Beasts

Heraldry evolved in medieval Europe as a way of formalizing the various emblems that noble families had adopted to proclaim their identity to a pre-literate population. Some families used geometrical designs, but many favoured animals which in some way echoed the family name or stood for some of the qualities they felt themselves to possess. Some of these animals were mythical, owing their existence to the incomplete knowledge of natural history in the medieval world: others, though based on exotic animals – such as lions, leopards and tigers – closely resembled more familiar, European creatures, such as wolves or dogs. Heraldic beasts made their appearances on shields, on the crests of helmets, and in wood and stone carvings.

The Unicorn
This mythical beast has always had a purely symbolic function, representing the lunar and feminine aspect and also, through the rampant horn, the victory of male over female. In heraldry it usually counterbalances the extrovert power of the lion.

The Horse
The horse appears prominently in heraldry in its prancing (invicta) form, symbolizing speed, power and nobility. In the Christian tradition it represents courage, while in the East it stands for fire and the heavens. The black horse is a herald of death.

The Eagle
Along with the falcon, the eagle represents the sky god, the power that rises above the world of men and, with acute vision, sees and comprehends all things.

The Griffin
A symbolic guardian of the path to salvation or of the tree of life, the griffin represents vigilance and vengeance. It combines the attributes of eagle (air) and lion (fire).

The Cockerel
In heraldry the cockerel represents pride and courage. Waking at dawn, it is a solar symbol, a sign of resurrection.

The Lion
An emblem of valour, royalty, and protective power, the lion embodies the wisdom and energy of the animal kingdom.

Dogs and Wolves

In most cultures the dog is a propitious symbol, standing for loyalty, watchfulness, courage, and skill in the hunt. Dogs also symbolize masculinity, the sun, wind and fire, and in the Celtic tradition are associated with healing. Faithful in life, dogs were often sacrificed and buried in the tomb along with their masters: the Egyptians and Greeks believed that they shared the after-life with humans. Wolves and foxes are symbolically ambivalent. The fox often symbolizes cunning and deceit, although native North Americans credit it with great instinctive wisdom. In the Christian tradition, wolves represent cruelty, devouring those sheep who refuse the protection of the good shepherd; but for the Romans the she-wolf who suckled Romulus and Remus was held to symbolize maternal care.

The Fox
In Oriental mythology, the fox was a powerfully positive symbol, representing longevity for the Japanese and serving as the magical messenger of the rice god Inari. The Chinese credit the fox with the power to change shape and even assume human form.

Anubis
The Egyptian guardian of the dead, Anubis took the form of the jackal. Under his care, the soul was assured safe passage to the judgment seat of Osiris, lord of the underworld and the heavens.

The Werewolf
Man by day, beast and devourer of the unwary by night, the werewolf – whose origins lie in medieval Europe – is a potent symbol of fear, and of the violence that lurks under the veneer of civilization.

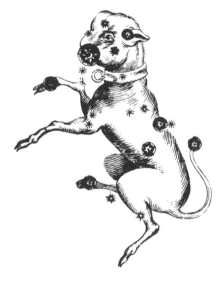

Canis Major
The ancients saw the dog in the night sky as the constellation of Canis Major: the so-called "dog days" were the languid days of high summer in the Mediterranean world, heralded by the rising of the dog star.

Cats

Nocturnal and independent, the cat is a less virile symbol than the dog, being lunar rather than solar, and endowed with the hidden mysteries of the female rather than with the more open strengths of the male. The cat was domesticated by the ancient Egyptians around 2,000BC, and came to represent Bastet, the moon goddess, as well as other deities. The Chinese credited the cat with the ability to banish evil spirits, although its entry into a house was seen as an omen of poverty. In the West, the cat represented Satan, lust and darkness, and its best-known symbolic appearance is as the black familiar of the witch. In their more favourable aspect, cats were seen as rain-makers, perhaps owing to their acute sensitivity to water.

Bastet
With its fixity of gaze, the cat symbolized watchfulness to the Egyptians. It stood for Bastet, the moon goddess, who coldly and calmly surveyed the doings of men and beasts.

The Jaguar's Eyes
South American Indians believed that the mirrored eyes of the jaguar were a conduit to the realm of spirits. Shamans claimed to see the future through a jaguar's eyes.

Cats
Cats can stand for domesticity, but are also used to represent cruelty (perhaps because of their hunting habits) and liberty (since they are difficult to catch). In the Celtic world, cats symbolized evil and were used in ritual sacrifice.

The Tiger
Particularly revered in China, the tiger symbolized ferocity and protectiveness, and images of it often adorned gateposts and entrances to buildings. Considered to be king of the beasts, it represented vitality and animal energy.

Birds and Flight

Flight has always represented freedom from the physical restrictions of earth-bound life, and the ascent of the soul to the gods, either through mystical experience or through death. Birds share something of the same symbolic meaning, but because they come from the skies they can also assume the role of messengers from higher powers, whether for good or ill. They are linked with tree symbolism. One dark- and one light-coloured bird in the branches of the tree of life represent the dual nature of reality (darkness and light, life and death). In a Hindu variant of this image, one bird eats the tree's fruit while the other watches, symbolizing the active approach to life contrasting with the contemplative.

When associated with serpents, birds signify conflict, the battle between sky (open, spacious) and sea (deep, hidden). Psychologists interpret this as the conflict between the conscious and the unconscious, or between exoteric and esoteric knowledge.

Icarus
In Greek myth, Icarus and his father Daedalus escaped imprisonment on Crete by flying away on wings attached to their shoulders with wax. Ignoring his father's advice, Icarus flew too close to the sun, whereupon the wax melted and he fell to his death. He represents the lapse from grace of those driven too hard by ambition.

The Pelican
The belief that the pelican feeds its young with its own blood made it a symbol of self-sacrifice (and, in Christianity, of Christ). In alchemy it is the antithesis of the raven (which stands for the stage of dying to the world), and thus represents resurrection.

Feathers
For the Celts, the feathered cloak conferred on the wearer some of the qualities of the bird – lightness, speed and the ability to travel to other worlds. For the native North Americans, feathers were symbolic of the Great Spirit and of the sun.

The Bird of Ill Omen
The raven is credited with the gift of prophecy, often of an unwelcome kind. In the Middle Ages, it was a symbol of mortality: among native North Americans it was held to be wise and sly.

The Ba
A bird is often seen as a symbol for the flight of the soul from the grave. The Egyptians, gifted in combining human and animal imagery, depicted it as the Ba – a hawk with a human head.

Leda and the Swan
In Greek myth, Zeus took the form of a swan to seduce Leda, Queen of Sparta (above), and the swan therefore came to symbolize love and the gods. It also stands for solitude, music and poetry, and its whiteness represents sincerity.

The Peacock
In Christian art the peacock represents immortality. Persian symbolism holds that two peacocks around the tree of life stand for man's psychic duality. In the Buddhist tradition, the bird's "hundred-eyed tail" is a symbol of compassionate watchfulness.

Fishes and Shells

The fish and the shell are universally positive in meaning. Many cultures see the fish as a symbol of fecundity and of the life-giving properties of water. Fish represent life in the depths (deep water is held to symbolize the unconscious) and thus stand for inspiration and creativity. The first letters of the Greek words *Iesous Christos Theou Huios Soter* (Jesus Christ, Son of God, Saviour) make *Ichthus*, the Greek word for fish, and throughout Christian tradition there is a strong symbolic association of Christ with fish. For example, the apostles were called "fishers of men". In Buddhism, the fish symbolizes freedom from the restraints of desire and attachment. The Hindu gods Brahma and Vishnu were said to appear sometimes in fish form. Unlike the fish, which is phallic and masculine, the shell is universally feminine, standing for birth, good fortune and resurrection.

The Birth of Venus
The association between the scallop and the goddess Venus is the theme of this painting by Sandro Botticelli. According to myth, Venus was born from the foam produced when the severed genitals of Uranus were cast into the sea, and was carried ashore on a scallop shell. Along with other bivalves (hinged shells), the scallop represents the female genitalia and the feminine principle. The scallop is also the symbol of Christian pilgrimage (specifically to the shrine of Saint James in the Spanish city of Santiago de Compostela) and initiation, because it was used to scoop up the baptismal waters.

The Salmon
Associated in Celtic mythology with prophecy and inspiration because of its instinct to find its distant spawning grounds.

Three Fishes
Sometimes intertwined and sometimes sharing a single head, the three fishes symbolize the Trinity in Christian belief. Just as fish move through the water undetected by all except those with keen eyes, so the divine forces are visible only to those with good spiritual sight.

The Draught of Fishes (left)
The symbol of abundance and wisdom: St. Luke's account of the miracle of the draught of fishes predicts Peter's later role as a fisher of men. The net is also used as a symbol of mankind's attempts to capture enlightenment.

Jonah and the Whale (above)
The whale initially symbolized the power of the cosmic waters: only later did it acquire negative connotations, representing the jaws and belly of Hell. Jonah, when swallowed by the whale, emerges three days later, symbolizing rebirth through spiritual conversion.

The Octopus (right)
One of the commonest symbols among Mediterranean civilizations, the octopus is related to the spiral and represents the unfolding of creation from the mystic centre. Along with the crab, it is sometimes associated with the astrological sign of Cancer.

The Conch (above)
In Buddhism, the sound of the conch symbolizes the voice of Buddha. In Hindu belief the conch is sacred to Vishnu, and symbolizes the call to awaken from ignorance.

Monkeys and Elephants

Monkeys and elephants figure extensively in Eastern symbolism. The monkey, which appears to chatter incessantly and fruitlessly, represents the distracted mind that must be focused by practices such as meditation: when tamed, the monkey is capable of great loyalty and intelligence.

The symbolism of the elephant derives from the animal's important role in civil and commercial life. Traditionally the vehicle for princes and maharajahs who rode high upon its back, the elephant represents status, strength and foresight. Because of its longevity, it stands for victory over death, and wisdom and dignity in old age.

Three Mystic Monkeys
Monkeys represent our tendency to spread gossip and to gloat over the misfortunes of others. The three mystic monkeys – See No Evil, Hear No Evil, Speak No Evil – symbolize our ability to rise above this debased state, and to control and discipline our minds.

The White Elephant
The white elephant is sacred in Buddhism because the Buddha is said to have entered his mother's womb in this form: the animal therefore stands for the Buddha's patience, wisdom and long memory. To the Chinese, the elephant is one of the power animals, symbolizing cosmic energy.

Hanuman (left)
The Indian monkey god, a hero of *The Ramayana* (where he is an ally of Rama, an incarnation of Vishnu), symbolizes cunning and strength. When fire is sent against him, he tames it, symbolizing the Tantric power to transform even the fiercest emotions into spiritual energy.

Ganesha (above)
In the Hindu religion, the elephant is the vehicle of Ganesha, god of sacred wisdom, invincibility and prudence. Ganesha is a patron of learning, and the legendary scribe who wrote the *Mahabharata*. He is traditionally shown as an elephant, usually upright and with four arms to confer gifts and protection upon the human race.

Sheep and Goats

For many in the West, the goat is primarily a symbol of Satan and magic, but outside the Judeo–Christian tradition it enjoys a more positive image. In ancient Greece it was sacred to Zeus (who as an infant was suckled by the she-goat Amalthea), while its fecundity and cunning rendered it sacred also to Pan and Artemis. Perhaps because of its mountain home, the goat in the Hindu tradition symbolized superiority and the higher self. In Norse legend Thor's chariot was pulled across the heavens by goats.

The sheep usually stands for the opposite – blindness and stupidity. However, its tendency to follow unquestioningly has also made it a symbol of the pupil who closely follows the teachings of a god or spiritual master, surrendering individual will in exchange for an enlightened view of the unitary nature of existence.

The Goat
This depiction of the goat as Devil by occultist Eliphas Lévi (see page 145) incorporates a range of magical symbolism. The caduceus rises from the genitals, the pentagram occupies the place of the third eye, the triple crown of fire adorns the head, the hands point to lunar symbols, and the horns and the breasts indicate the union of male and female powers.

The Sacrificial Lamb
A symbol of martyrdom. In the Feast of the Passover the blood of the lamb represents obedience to God's will.

The Good Shepherd
The symbol of care and protection for the helpless, the Good Shepherd is common to all formerly nomadic cultures.

Ea (Onnes)
Ea, the Babylonian god of the waters (also known as Onnes), is often portrayed as a goat–fish, a symbol uniting the fecundity of sea and land. This image, based on Sumerian pottery, shows Ea as a group of goats encircling a central symbol for water.

Bulls, Stags and Bears

To the modern mind the bull may seem an unambiguous representation of maleness, strength and procreative power. In Mithraic and Roman culture it was sacrificed at the turn of the year, its blood symbolizing the masculine essence that fertilized the feminine earth and returned life to the land. But the symbolism of the bull is actually not so clear-cut. The crescent shape of its horns has marked it as a lunar rather than a solar animal, particularly among the civilizations of the Mediterranean and the Near East. As such, it carries feminine connotations, and was attributed by the Romans to the goddess Venus.

Europa and the Bull
In Greek myth Zeus appeared as a white bull and carried off Europa (daughter of King Agenor of Tyre) who later bore him two sons, one of whom, Minos, became king of Crete. Christian interpretations of this myth saw the white bull as Christ, carrying the soul to heaven.

The Ox
The ox and buffalo share much of the symbolism of the bull, but achieve particular power as representatives of the ego in Taoism and Buddhism. The Taoist sage Lao Tzu is often shown riding a buffalo to indicate the possibility of taming the ego.

The Stag
Shamans have often been depicted dressed as stags, indicating the creature's role as a symbol of wisdom. In Mediterranean cultures the stag was identified with the tree of life (because of its branching antlers). For the Chinese the stag is a symbol of virility.

The Bear
In its male form the bear symbolized bravery and strength to the native North Americans and the Chinese. In its female form the Greeks saw it as sacred to Artemis, the goddess of the hunt (Diana in Roman myth).

Swine

Though exploited and reviled in the modern world, the pig has an honorable history, featuring prominently in the symbology of many civilizations. Owing to the large size of her litters and her numerous, productive mammary glands, the sow was a symbol of fertility throughout the ancient world. The Egyptians believed the white sow to be sacred to Isis, the great mother, while the black pig was attributed to Set, the sinister negative force within creation. In some Greek legends Zeus was suckled by a sow while in hiding from his father Cronos, and pigs were routinely sacrificed to Ceres and Demeter, goddesses of fertility. The Hindus also respected the sow, and held it to symbolize Vajravarahi, the feminine aspect of the god Vishnu (who himself was once incarnated as a boar).

The Buddhists saw the pig as a symbol of ignorance and greed, while in the Judaic tradition it represented unclean food (perhaps originally for good hygienic reasons). The Christians adopted the pig as a sign of sensuality and the sins of the flesh: in the New Testament Christ drives unclean spirits into the Gadarene swine, symbolizing the need for men and women to triumph over their lower natures.

The Pig as Gluttony
Gluttony, one of the seven deadly sins, was abhorred by the Christian Church because it strengthened the coarser, material side of human nature. Rather unfairly, the pig was chosen to symbolize gluttony, and this undoubtedly contributed to the debased image suffered by this intelligent animal today.

The Boar
A symbol of strength and courage: for the Celts it stood for magic and prophecy, because of its solitary life in the forest. In Western Europe, its head symbolized health and preservation from danger: hence its presence at feasts and as a crest on warriors' helmets.

The Sow and Litter
The sow is an appropriate symbol of motherhood, both in the context of fecundity and of maternal care. The native North Americans portrayed the pig as a rain-bearer, bringing life to the land for the benefit of all the children of the Great Spirit.

Lesser Creatures

While birds, domestic animals and large or conspicuous creatures have taken centre stage in the symbolic language of most cultures, lesser animals were also felt to play an important part in the magical world which our ancestors saw around them. Living close to nature, the ancients felt all things to be interconnected in an intricate web of being, and they attributed meaning to all aspects of nature. Consciousness was thought to pervade the whole of creation – the stars in the night sky, the wind in the trees, even the scurryings of the smallest creatures. The insects, whose behaviour and life cycles were poorly understood by the ancients, developed particularly rich symbolic associations. For example, flies were considered to be driven by demonic forces: Beelzebub, a name now synonymous with Satan, was originally a Syrian personification of the destructive power of swarming insects.

The Bat
In many cultures the bat embodied the powers of darkness and chaos. Buddhists saw it as a mark of the ignorant, distracted mind, but to the Chinese it represented long life and happiness.

The Toad
Often associated with witchcraft and the repulsive side of life. But like the serpent, the toad is often depicted with a jewel in its head, denoting the wisdom that sees the sacred in all things.

The Spider
For the Celts, the spider's web symbolized the web that held all life together. For Egyptians and Greeks it stood for fate. Christians believed the web to represent the snare of Satan. The spider itself stands for the Great Mother in her devouring aspect.

The Hare
Universally held to symbolize love, fertility, and the menstrual cycle. The hare has long been seen as a magical creature – its foot was often carried to ward off witches and evil. It is closely associated with the moon (some see a hare in the moon's contours).

Hybrid Creatures

Imaginary hybrid creatures have two main functions: they bring together the symbolic strengths of different animals; and, in the case of hybrids formed of two species from different elements, they represent the fundamental unity of existence. For example, the chimera – part lion, part goat, part serpent – symbolized the three divisions of the year – spring, summer and winter. To the minds that invented them, hybrids presented no inherent contradictions, because if all creation was interconnected, there was no reason why certain ingredients should not be permuted in new and different ways. There is much evidence that the ancients did not separate imagination and reality in the way that is habitual to us. If something could be imagined, there was a sense in which it must really exist.

In the great majority of cases, hybrid creatures carried a positive symbolic meaning. They inhabited a dimension that spanned this and other worlds, and thus could serve not only to help mankind in the struggle against dark forces but also to act as messengers from the gods and as sources of wisdom in themselves. Many Egyptian gods were portrayed as part-animal, part-human (see page 26), and throughout the ancient world there was an belief in the power of the gods to change their shape at will in order to influence the world of humankind.

Garuda
Half-man and half-eagle, Garuda serves in Hinduism as the vehicle of the god Vishnu, and in Tibetan Buddhism as destroyer of the *nagas* or evil-doers. Devotees of Vishnu use images of Garuda, the enemy of snakes, as their emblem. The ferocity of Garuda as portrayed in Indian and Tibetan art is intended to serve as a warning of retribution for the enemies of the natural order.

The Sphinx
The sphinx existed in Egyptian mythology long before its representation in stone beside the Great Pyramid of Cheops. With a human (often female) head, the body of a bull, the feet of a lion and the wings of an eagle, the sphinx combines the four creatures that symbolize the four elements. The sphinx had access to all wisdom, and symbolized the riddle of human existence.

The Basilisk
The most terrifying of mythical creatures, the basilisk occurs in legends of East and West as a symbol of evil, lust and disease (especially of syphilis in 15th-century Europe). Its gaze was lethal, and anyone who fought it had to do so while watching its reflection in a mirror.

The Satyr
Nature spirits and followers of Dionysus (the Greek god of ecstasy, wine and music), the satyrs were half men and half goats. They originally represented the amoral, lazy and pleasure-seeking sides of human nature, but were later identified, in Christian Europe, with the Devil.

The Chimera
Dating back to the 5th century BC, the chimera is an ancient symbol of elemental chaos and the dangers of land and sea. It was a portent of storms, shipwrecks and natural disasters, especially volcanic eruptions, and appears in medieval Christian art as a symbol of Satanic forces.

The Harpy

In Greek mythology, harpies were female wind spirits, associated with the underworld and the flight of the soul from the body. They had the ability to summon winds, causing storms on land and whirlpools at sea, and were believed to be responsible for sudden, unexpected deaths.

The Siren

The daughters of Poseidon, the Greek god of the sea, the sirens stood for feminine beauty in its most beguiling and destructive form. Depicted as birds with women's heads, they possessed beautiful voices which, heard above the sighing of the sea, lured mariners to their doom.

The Centaur

Part man, part horse, the centaur represents the wild, lawless, instinctual side of mankind. It is the antithesis of the knight, who rides (and therefore controls) the horse of the instincts. In Greek art, the centaurs were often shown ridden by Dionysus, an allusion to their amorous, drunken habits. However, Chiron, the gentlest of the centaurs, symbolized the healing powers of nature, and his skill with the bow represented nature's power and fertility.

The Mermaid

Sometimes thought to be hallucinations by sailors starved of female company, mermaids symbolize idealized, elusive feminine beauty, but also vanity and fickleness. Like all creatures of the deep, they stand for the unconscious, and in particular for the anima, the feminine aspect within the male psyche.

The Natural World

The direct experience of nature was the most powerful influence on the perceptions of the ancients. Their concepts of space and time, and of their own position in the universe, could be understood only in relation to the natural world, every aspect of which was believed to express a particular feature of divine energy. The earliest gods were, not surprisingly, embodiments of nature. Nearly all ancient cultures originally represented the earth and nature itself as a maternal goddess: Aranrhod (Celtic), Nekhebet (Egyptian), Nokomis (Algonquin) and Gaia (Greek) were all versions of the universal mother figure.

There was also a widespread belief that all forms of life were interchangeable, and that mankind was a part of nature, rather than its master. In depictions of the Mesopotamian shepherd god Dumuzi (Tammuz), plant, animal and human forms blend into one another.

Images of the tree-man (see page 103) occur in numerous Western cultures.

Although the primitive nature gods were often superseded by wider and more sophisticated pantheons, myths and symbols based on the natural world remained prominent in all cultures, and some were of worldwide significance. The relationship between the bird (a symbol of fire, purity and the spirit) and the serpent (the earth and underworld) is the subject of numerous myths. And the turtle is a symbol of the universe (the heavens, earth and underworld represented by its upper shell, body and lower shell) in both North America and Southern Asia. Depictions of the tree of life (see page 102) appear in nearly all cultures at all times, and this ancient symbol appears in modern Christianity as an emblem of the Virgin Mary, who gave the world her fruit, Jesus Christ.

The Chrysanthemum
In the East, the chrysanthemum was a propitious symbol, and also stood for contemplation and the onset of autumn.

The Mystical Garden
In this painting, by the visionary 19th-century
artist, Samuel Palmer, the garden represents the
enclosed, feminine principle.

Trees

The tree is one of mankind's most potent symbols. It is the embodiment of life, the point of union of the three realms (heaven, earth and water), and a world axis around which the entire universe is organized. Ancient peoples widely believed the tree to be infused with an abundance of divine creative energy (often personalized in the form of supernatural creatures) which could be consciously harnessed by the adept, allowing access to other states of being. Forests came to symbolize mystery and transformation, and were home to sorcerers and enchanters.

Tree worship was widespread in nearly all parts of the globe where the climate was favourable to tree growth. Some tree symbols are virtually worldwide. For example, evergreens universally stand for longevity and immortality, while deciduous trees represent regeneration and rebirth: in their own way, both serve to reassure men and women of their own continuing existence.

However, in general, individual species acquired their own, culture-specific significance. The oak was revered by the Celtic and Norse peoples, while in ancient Greece the elder was considered sacred to Pan, the ivy to Bacchus, the bay to Apollo, the laurel to Dionysus. In Egypt the tamarisk was sacred to Osiris. In ancient China, trees in the vicinity of tombs or temples were protected as it was believed that the spirits of the dead and of the gods resided in them.

Many trees were believed to have healing properties because they symbolized specific illnesses. Thus, since the aspen trembles in the wind, it was used in the treatment of fevers. Hazel was thought to possess magical powers, and was used for water divining and to make the magician's wand. Wood itself also carried symbolic meaning and was thought in the Middle East and India to represent the *prima materia*, the fundamental material from which all things were made.

The Palm Tree
Tall with radiating foliage, the palm tree suggests the sun and therefore came to represent fame, victory and righteousness. Palm leaves were funerary emblems symbolizing the after-life.

The Pine Cone
With its flame-like shape and erect appearance on the tree, the pine cone was for the Greeks a sign of masculinity. The Romans held it to be a symbol of purity, sacred to Venus.

The Christmas Tree
In the winter solstice celebrations of Scandinavian and other North European peoples, the decorated evergreen symbolizes the life-force that persists even in the dead months of the year.

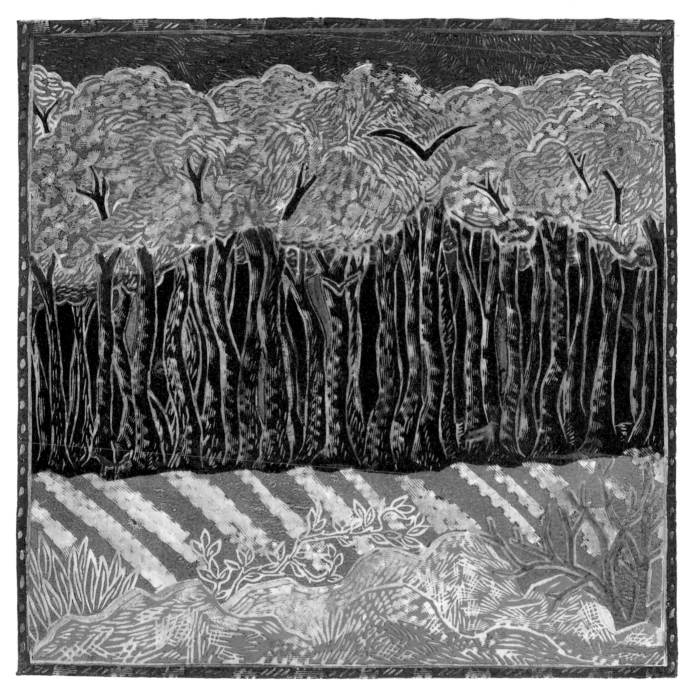

The Forest

The symbolic interpretation of the forest is ancient, dating back to the time when landscapes were heavily wooded and clearance for agriculture was an arduous task. The forest is a place of darkness, chaos and uncertainty, in contrast to the order and openness of cultivated land. To those who show no fear, however, it may be a place of peace and refuge. Psychologically, it is a symbol of the unconscious, where there are secrets to be discovered and perhaps dark emotions and memories to be faced.

The Tree of Life
Standing at the centre of Paradise, the Tree of Life is a representation of perfect harmony. The twelve (sometimes ten) fruit in the branches are the rewards of spiritual growth – among these are wisdom, love, truth and beauty. The fruits are manifestations of the sun. Immortality is given to those who eat them, or drink an essence extracted from the tree itself.

The World Tree
With its roots around the earth and its branches in the heavens, the World Tree symbolizes the potential ascent of humankind from the dense realm of matter to the rarified reaches of the spirit. A notable version of this symbol isYggdrasil, the Scandinavian Cosmic Tree, from which the Nordic god Odin hung and suffered for nine days and nights.

The Inverted Tree
The Inverted Tree has its roots in the spiritual world and grows down towards the Earth. It symbolizes the creative power of the spirit, as well as the belief that human life is the descent of spirit into bodily form. This symbol was used by magicians: the example here is a Kabbalistic Tree of Life showing the sefiroth – the ten aspects of God.

Two Trees, One Root
The esoteric traditions teach that the differences of the physical world stem from an original state of oneness. The aspirant on the spiritual path must gather together the fragmented pieces of his or her own true nature. The two trunks from one root show duality emerging from unity, yet retaining their oneness in the reality that underlies appearances.

Tree as Woman

Outwardly this image symbolizes the Earth Mother, the nurturing feminine principle. But inwardly it is also the invisible life-force slumbering within the Earth until inseminated by the masculine energy of the wind, rain and sun.

The Tree of Knowledge (right)

This is a dualistic symbol, embodying the knowledge of good and evil. Tempted to taste the fruit, Adam and Eve were doomed to the world of opposites. In addition to its familiar role as Tempter, the serpent entwined around the tree is an ancient mystical symbol of earth energy rising. The Tree of Knowledge is also depicted as a vine.

Specific trees (above)

Different species of tree carry their own symbolic meaning in both Eastern and Western cultures. For the Celts and pre-Celtic Druids, the oak represented both divinity and the masculine principle, while for the Romans it was the emblem of Jupiter, lord of thunder. The fig tree was a Buddist symbol of enlightenment. In Chinese Taoist tradition, the peach tree stood for immortality.

Tree as Man

This is one of the most powerful fertility symbols, representing the male energy which impregnates the earth with life but is itself subject to the eternal cycle of decay and renewal. Sometimes referred to as the Green Man, the symbol recurs across Western cultures, appearing as various figures from the god Pan to Herne the Hunter.

Flowers and Plants

The Greeks believed that paradise was carpeted with asphodels. The Chinese imagined that for each woman living in this world, a flower bloomed in the next. These two ancient beliefs exemplify the most common symbolic meanings of the flower: the paradisal state and feminine beauty. The opening of the flower from the bud represents creation (the manifestation of energy moving outward from the centre) and the energy of the sun. Flowers are universal symbols of youth and vitality, but because of their impermanence they also connote fragility.

Plants represent the cycle of life (fertility, death and rebirth) and many were thought to thrive on the life-force (body or blood) of a particular god: the ancient Egyptians believed that wheat grew from the body of Osiris. Many herbs were considered sacred, some because of their medicinal properties and others because their growth habit or appearance suggested a link with the gods or mankind (for example, the mandrake's roots resemble the human body).

The Mandrake
The human-shaped mandrake root was believed to have great curative powers and was widely used in sorcerers' potions (it is now known to contain several poisonous hallucinogens). In Hebrew tradition it symbolized fertility and was eaten to aid conception.

Mistletoe
Mistletoe was taken to symbolize the female in relation to the maleness of the oak tree in whose branches it grew. Neither a tree nor a shrub, and without roots in the ground, it was held to have a special relationship to the divine, standing for the state beyond earthly limitations.

The Rose
In Christianity, the red rose can symbolize the Virgin Mother or the blood shed by Jesus on the cross. It represents secrecy (confessionals are often adorned with a five-petalled rose). Three roses are a potent masonic symbol, representing light, love and life.

The Garland
Combining the symbolism of the flower and the ring, the garland represents variously good luck, holiness, fertility and initiation. It also stands for the binding together of this world and the next (a significance still evident today in the funerary wreath).

Garlic
Like its relative the lily, garlic is a symbol of the higher world, partly because of its association with lightning (its scent is said to be similar to the smell caused by the discharge of lightning).

The Lotus
Growing in mud at the bottom of a pond, the lotus flower raises itself above the water and reveals its beauty. It thus stands for the soul rising from the confusion of matter into the clarity of enlightenment.

The Garden
A symbol of nature under control and of the human soul which, like the garden, must be cared for and cultivated. The garden also stands for paradise, and the Fields of the Blessed. In India, gardens sometimes take the form of mandalas (see page 60).

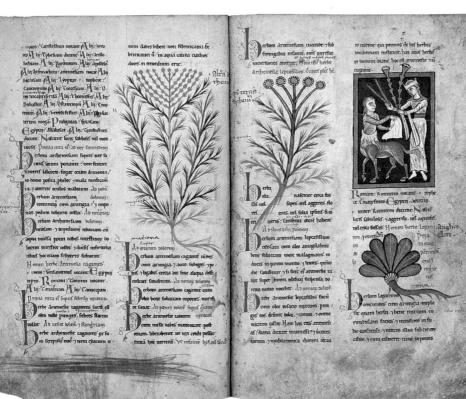

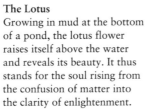

Herbs
The symbolic meanings of herbs, like those of many other plants, grow out of their individual properties. For example, rue, rosemary and thyme symbolize repentance, remembrance and purity respectively: rue has the bitterness of repentance, rosemary carries a scent which endures like memory, and thyme was thought useful in purifying the taste of food.

Food and Drink

Food has many positive overtones: it connotes fertility, abundance and celebration, but is most often linked with peace and the resolution of differences. This association stems from a belief that food is imbued with a life-force that puts men and women in touch with the source of primal energy, creating a universal fellowship. Certain foods, such as those made from corn, were especially symbolic in this sense: in many cultures it was considered a breach of natural law to harm a person with whom one had broken bread.

Drink is also potently symbolic. Water, the primordial fluid, suggests life and purity, while milk represents the sustaining compassion of the earth and of motherhood. Wine is linked with blood and sacrifice: in the Eucharist its mixture with water symbolizes Christ's dual nature (God and mankind). Because of its power to alter consciousness, wine also symbolized ecstatic union with the gods.

Honey
Together with milk, honey symbolizes the abundance of the Promised Land of the Jews. Because of its preservative and aphrodisiac qualities, it stands for immortality or fertility.

Sheaves of Corn
A symbol of the fertility of the earth and the inner fertility of the enlightened mind. Ears of corn are believed to be the offspring of the sun and the earth. The Eleusinian mysteries (a series of initiations into divine wisdom held in ancient Greece) were symbolized by ears of corn.

Mushrooms and Toadstools
The mushroom is the Chinese symbol for happiness and rebirth, and was believed to be the food of the Taoist immortals. In Western folklore, toadstools are the homes of elves and pixies, and because of their phallic shape, were associated with fertility and sexual potency.

The Pomegranate
In ancient Greece, the pomegranate was the symbol of Persephone and of the return of life in spring. With its countless seeds, the fruit stood for fertility and the unity in diversity of all creation. In the Christian tradition, the pomegranate symbolized the boundless love of the Creator.

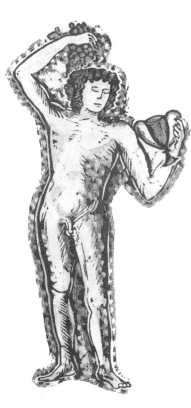

Dionysus

The Greek god of wine, happiness and agriculture, Dionysus
implies the union of heaven and earth, of spirituality and sensuality.
In one legend he was killed and eaten by the Titans, who were in
turn burnt by Zeus. Mankind was set the task of finding Dionysus
among the ashes – symbolic of the search for our true identity.

The Last Supper

Many sacred traditions carry accounts of god-kings who undergo
ritual death for their people. The Last Supper elevates this sacrifice
to a spiritual meal, and when repeated in the Eucharist the bread
and wine symbolize (or for some actually become) the body and
blood of Christ.

The Peach

In China the peach is symbolically linked with marriage,
immortality and longevity. Shou-lao, the god of long life, is often
shown emerging from, or holding, a peach from the tree in the
gardens of Paradise which bears fruit once every 3,000 years.

The Golden Apple

The golden apple represents discord, since its presentation by Paris
to Aphrodite in a divine beauty contest led indirectly to the Trojan
War. Freyja, the Norse goddess of love and magic, gave apples of
immortality from her garden to rejuvenate the gods.

The Elements

The elements were believed by the ancients to be the essential energy forces that sustain the world. In the West they are four in number – fire, water, air and earth. The Chinese classified metal as a separate element, while in India and Tibet a spiritual element (the "ether") was thought to permeate and vivify the other four. The central importance of the elements as organizing principles in the universe is a constant in the symbology of all cultures. Practitioners of alchemy developed a shorthand form of representing the elements based on the geometry of the triangle (see below): for example, because fire always moves skyward, it is represented by an upward-pointing triangle. The elements were seen as vital components of the human body, and the maintenance of physical and psychological health was a matter of keeping a balance between them, just as a balance was needed in the outside world.

The Human Body
Composed of the four elements plus the invisible spiritual dimension, the (male) body was the universal symbol for life in all its forms, the link between heaven and earth, and the personification of the energy of the gods.

The Sylph
Spirits of the air, the insubstantial sylphs were believed to be in communion with the divine.

The Salamander
In Western traditions, the salamander was believed to be the spirit and guardian of fire, and to live in a volcano.

The Ondine
The spirit of water, usually represented as a graceful young woman, is at once captivating and treacherous.

The Gnome
The mischievous spirit of the earth, associated by some with the underworld, needed to be appeased with offerings.

Air

Isis
The greatest of the Egyptian goddesses and possessed of immense magical powers, Isis is the divine mother and protector. She is often depicted as a kite, a form that she assumed to search for the dismembered body of her brother Osiris. Later, after reassembling the body, she used her wings to revivify him with the breath of life.

The Sailing Ship
All the great seafaring civilizations had gods or saints (Aeolus in the Greek and Saint Nicholas in the Christian world) who controlled the winds, and to whom prayers were offered before a voyage.

Prana
Many Eastern philosophies hold that the body's vital energies are carried in the air. This elemental energy (symbolized by the central glyph above) is called *prana* by the Indians, *chi* by the Chinese and *ki* by the Japanese. It circulates through the body along what are now called the acupuncture meridians, and can be controlled by means of yogic exercises in order to improve bodily health, gain psychic powers and transmute physical energy into spiritual.

Pegasus
Pegasus, the winged horse that sprang from the blood of Medusa after her beheading by Perseus, symbolizes mankind's desire to take to the air, as well as the capricious nature of the element. The taming of Pegasus by Bellerophon (aided by Athene's bridle) shows that, with the help of the gods, mankind can tame the elements.

Fire

The Phoenix
Half eagle, half pheasant, the phoenix occurs in Central American, Eastern and European myth. It sets itself alight every hundred years, only to rise rejuvenated from the ashes after three days, symbolizing resurrection, immortality, and mankind's indestructible spirit.

Agni
An important early Hindu god, Agni is usually shown riding a ram (a symbol of solar energy) and with seven tongues (the mystic number of creation). He was traditionally appeased with gifts of melted butter, which he was believed to lick up with his seven tongues.

Incense
In the East, incense is believed to offer protection against evil spirits. It is linked with purity and the ascent of the spirit toward the heavens.

Smoke
In native North American culture, smoke symbolizes peace and the path followed at death. It sometimes stands for ignorance (vision obscured).

The Ship Burial
In Scandinavia the bodies of Viking chiefs were cremated in longships, the rising smoke representing a return of the spirit to the sun, the giver of life.

Prometheus
In Greek myth, Prometheus stole fire (a symbol of the wisdom that differentiates divinity from mankind) from the gods, concealed it in a hollow staff, and brought it to earth. He symbolizes the courage needed to challenge the decree of the gods.

The Lantern
The shadows cast by an illuminated, decorated lantern were considered in the East to have an independent existence of their own. Lanterns were therefore used to project auspicious symbols during celebrations.

The Firecracker
In China, firecrackers are believed to bring luck and to frighten demons. They are set off in groups of three to honour the gods of health, wealth and longevity.

Water

Rivers

As the life-source and communication routes of ancient civilizations, rivers carry potent meanings. They represent the boundaries between countries or between life and death. In Hindu belief, rivers symbolize purification (the Ganges can wash away all shortcomings). They can also connote the passing of time.

Steam

Water ascending as steam is the transformation of the material into the spiritual. Native North American tribes believed that steam possessed the combined purifying powers of fire and water, and used it in the Sweat Lodge ceremony, which represented the cleansing and revivifying of body, mind and spirit.

Streams

Streams share some of the significance of rivers, but are closer to the creative source and therefore represent life and the "stream of consciousness" within which mankind lives. Four streams were said to flow from the foot of the Tree of Life in Paradise, carrying the life-force to the four corners of the world.

Wells

Water typically moves down toward earth. Its emergence *from* the earth is usually taken to represent a sacred gift from the womb of the Earth Mother herself. In the Islamic tradition, wells can stand for Paradise. Traditionally female, many are also credited with the power to heal or to grant wishes.

Boats and Rafts

The boat or raft symbolizes a safe passage across to the other shore. To the pure in heart, water presents no danger. Christ walked on the water, and many cultures have legends of holy men and women using the most unlikely craft with complete safety. Saint Patrick, the patron saint of Ireland, is said to have used a stone raft, while Bodhidharma (above), who brought Zen Buddhism to China, crossed the Yangtze on a hollow reed.

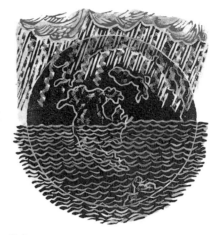

Ice and Snow
Ice symbolizes sterility, coldness and
rigidity, in humans and in nature. The
melting of ice therefore heralds the return
of life. Snow shares something of this
symbolic meaning; however, being soft and
beautiful, it also stands for latent truth and
hidden wisdom.

Clouds and Mist
Clouds symbolize mystery and the sacred:
in many cultures, the gods are shown
enveloped in cloud. The Chinese believed
that clouds were formed from the union of
yin and yang (see page 129), and therefore
symbolized peace. For the Romans, the
British Isles, shrouded in mist, symbolized
the magical land at the end of the world.

Rain
As a life-giving blessing from heaven, rain
has always symbolized divine favour and
revelation, the descent of grace upon the
earth. However, a deluge may be caused by
the wrath of the gods or the desire to purge
the earth of corruption. The innocent, of
course, may perish with the guilty.

Poseidon
Poseidon (Roman Neptune),
the brother of Zeus, originally
symbolized the cosmic power
fertilizing the sea, and for this
reason he is always shown
with the trident (representing
three, the number of creation).
Later he came to stand for the
power of the sea, and was
credited with the ability to
grant or withhold safe passage
to mariners. He was a violent
god, believed to be responsible
for earthquakes.

Earth

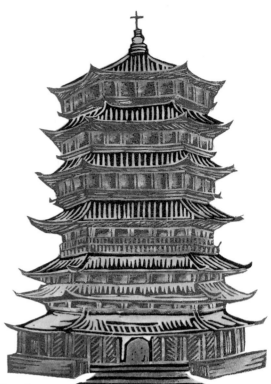

The Volcano
To those who live in their shadow, volcanoes are terrifying examples of the earth's destructive energy. The Persians associated them with Ahriman, the destructive force within the universe, who was shackled at the core of the earth to await the day of judgment. In Greek myth, volcanic activity was a sign that Hephaestos, the smith god, was busy in his workshop.

The Pagoda
Probably a development of the Buddhist stupa (see page 59), the Japanese pagoda represents ascent to heaven, and traditionally has seven stories to mark the stages of this ascent. It also stands for Mount Meru, the world axis at the centre of the universe.

The Valley
This protective, feminine symbol is associated with fertility, cultivation and water. In the Chinese and Christian traditions, the valley is linked with darkness and the unknown.

The Mountain
The meeting-places of heaven and earth, mountains symbolize masculinity, eternity, and ascent from animal to spiritual nature. Mountain tops are traditionally the home of the weather gods.

The Cave
The cave is a feminine symbol, and carries a range of meanings. It can represent the heart of the world, the unconscious, the entrance to the underworld, initiation, or esoteric wisdom.

Rainbows

To the ancients, who believed that all celestial phenomena were signs of divine activity, the appearance of a rainbow in the wake of a fierce storm signified the presence of a benign deity. Because it appeared to span the divide between the heavens and the earth, the rainbow was a particularly potent symbol of divine communication. The Incas associated the rainbow with their sun god, while in ancient Greece it was personified by the winged goddess Iris, who carried messages from the gods on Mount Olympus to the mortals below. Her benevolence extended to the gods (to whom she gave ambrosia and nectar), as well as to mortals (it was Iris who persuaded the Winds to fan the funeral pyre of the hero Patroclus, who perished in the Trojan war). In the Christian world, the rainbow symbolizes God's forgiveness and his covenant with mankind, because it appeared in the sky after Noah's ark came to rest on dry land following the deluge (see page 24). The positive associations of the rainbow are also evident in European folklore, which maintains that a crock of gold can be found where it meets the earth.

In the myths of numerous cultures, the rainbow is a metaphorical bridge between this world and that of the gods. For example, the Norse gods are said to have built a rainbow bridge called Bifrost between their dwelling-place, Asgard, and the earth. And in Chinese tradition, the rainbow is a symbol of the sky dragon, the union between heaven and earth

The Rainbow Body
In the Hindu and Buddhist Tantric traditions, the rainbow body is the highest meditative state attainable. The four elements that make up the body dissolve symbolically into rainbow light, and earthly life is shown to be truly insubstantial.

The Rainbow
In some African societies, the rainbow is equated with the sky serpent, a benificent symbol of energy flowing between heaven and earth. The kings and priests of the Bantu-speaking peoples of the Nilo-Saharan region justified their elevated position in society by inventing myths, in which they claimed to be descended from rainbows.

Thunder and Lightning

Thunder and lightning were once almost universally interpreted as manifestations of the gods, and most commonly as expressions of divine wrath. The Chinese goddess Tien Mu was the embodiment of lightning, whose task was to illuminate evil doers so that they could be struck down by the thunder god, Lei Kung. Native North Americans attributed thunder and lightning to the universal spirit, the Thunderbird, and in European folklore, thunder was thought to be the sound of giant bowls rolling along the heavens as the gods engaged in sport. When, in Greek myth, Semele asked Zeus to come to her undisguised, he appeared as a bolt of lightning and she was consumed by fire. Such symbolism was incorporated into Judeo-Christian belief, in which thunder and lightning signified God's direct presence. However, these phenomena were not invariably connected with divine assertiveness: in arid regions, when accompanied by rain, they represented fertility and vitality.

Lightning
Lightning has always been associated with intuition and inspiration. In the shamanic tradition, to be struck by lightning was a mark of initiation, while to be killed by it was to be taken directly to the heavens. In the West, some believe that being struck by lightning awakens latent psychic powers.

Thor
The Norse god of thunder caused the heavens to rumble as he rode across them in his wagon, and hurled his hammer to produce thunderbolts. A hammer symbol is believed to protect houses from fire.

The Dorje
This is the Tibetan Buddhist thunderbolt sceptre used in rituals and magical ceremonies. It represents male energy, its two globes symbolizing the meeting of heaven and earth.

The Shaman Mask
Shamans often dressed in animal skins to enhance their powers, but are also depicted in the zigzag shape of the lightning flash, symbolizing their ability to cross the bridge dividing the worlds.

Day and Night

In Christian, Buddhist and Islamic cultures, light is an aspect of divinity and kingship, and daytime is associated with divine activity and creation, as in the "seven days" in which God created the world and the "day of Brahma", the aeons-long cycle of manifestations of the Hindu creator god. In the Hindu religion, day (symbolizing spirit) and night (representing matter) are believed to be brought about by the opening and closing of Shiva's eyes. In European cultures, day generally stands for life and night for death, with the dawn corresponding to resurrection and joy. Some Renaissance thinkers saw both night and day as facets of the same process – the inexorable march of time. In this tradition, both carried negative connotations, standing for ageing, decay and death; they were sometimes depicted as two rats, one white, one black.

Night was the time when the spirits of the dead walked the earth and the "powers of darkness" (including Satan, the prince of darkness) were abroad. In Christian Europe, adherents of pagan religions were forced to perform their rituals covertly at night in order to avoid persecution. This reinforced the negative symbolism of night. As late as the 17th century it was held that diseases were more readily contracted at night, and tales of the nocturnal transformations of men and women into werewolves and vampire bats were widely believed. But night was not universally negative: it could stand for rest from the toils of the day, and for the womb of mother nature, which opened to readmit her children after sunset. In Greek mythology, the goddess Nyx was the personification of night. Often depicted wearing a star-spangled veil and black robe, she was the bringer of sleep, dreams and sexual pleasure, but in her negative aspect was feared even by the gods, being the mother of Moros (doom), Thanatos (death) and Hypnos (sleep).

Sleep
Many cultures regard sleep as a time when the soul leaves the body and travels in other levels of reality, bringing back memories as dreams. To the Tibetans, however, sleep is a rehearsal for death.

The Flaming Cauldron
In the Zoroastrian faith, the flaming cauldron is the symbol of Ahura Mazda, bringer of light, who is engaged in a continual struggle with Ahriman, the creator of evil and of night.

The Nurse of the Gods
In Greek and Mesopotamian culture, the nurse of the gods represents both the dawn and the ending of time. The two children cradled in her arms symbolize the link between sleep (white) and death (black).

Jewels and Precious Metals

Decorative and durable, jewels and precious metals have been used for centuries as talismans and amulets, and have acquired rich symbolic associations. Alchemy, for example, is centred on the quest for the philosopher's stone which will turn base metals into gold (see pages 146–151), and in astrology, each sign of the zodiac has an associated birthstone, which symbolizes the attributes of the sign.

A horde of gold and jewels hidden in a cave guarded by a dragon or serpent commonly represents the spiritual wisdom buried in the unconscious. In many religions a gem signifies a particular deity or holy person: in Christianity, for example, quartz stands for the Virgin Mary. Cut gemstones symbolize the revelation of the soul after the dross of the body has been chipped away: the sparkling facets denote the soul's reflection of the divine light. But gemstones can also have nega-tive connotations. In Christian myth, they were formed when Lucifer fell from heaven, his angelic light shattering into millions of lustrous fragments that stand for the inherent evil of material possessions.

Gold and jewels can also denote the wiles of the enchanter. Fairies used gold and rubies to entice mortals away from home and family at night; tragically for the victims, the treasure turned into the dead leaves of human vanity in the cold light of day. The ambivalence of gem symbolism is exemplified in the Eastern belief that jewels were formed from the saliva of snakes, representing both venom and spiritual wisdom.

In many traditions of East and West, it was believed that gold and silver were solidifications of solar and lunar energies respectively. Gold remains always untarnished, like the sun, while silver is subject to imperfections, like the face of the moon.

Lapis Lazuli
Particularly prized as a mark of divine favour, success and talent, lapis lazuli is also associated with unselfish love and compassion. For the Chinese, the stone symbolized vision and the power to cure diseases of the eye. In the ancient civilizations of Mesopotamia, lapis lazuli symbolized the firmament, and was used to decorate the ceilings of temples.

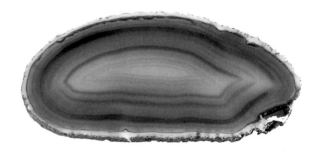

Agate
A symbol of worldly success and happiness, agate also attracts sympathy for the wearer. Black agate stands for courage, prosperity and vigour, red agate for health, longevity and spirituality.

The Pearl
Because of its pale, shimmering hue, the pearl has lunar, and therefore feminine, associations. Its origin in the sea within the shell of an oyster has caused it to be linked with hidden knowledge and esoteric wisdom. Pearls also symbolize patience, purity and peace, and owing to their translucent quality they can stand for tears of sorrow or joy.

Gold and Silver
Revered for its incorruptibility, gold is a near-universal symbol of the sun, divine illumination, purity, masculinity, immortality and wisdom. In ancient Egypt, it was the tangible presence of the gods in the material. The Aztecs saw gold as the excrement of the sun god, the Chinese Taoists as the essence of heaven. Silver, a lunar, feminine symbol, stands for virginity and eloquence (the silver tongue). When polished, silver represents the soul cleansed of sin: it is ambivalent mainly in Christianity, in which pieces of silver symbolized Christ's betrayal.

Jade
The most precious of all stones to the Chinese, for whom it symbolized the perfection, immortality and magical powers embodied in the emperor: heaven was often depicted as a perforated jade disk. Each colour of jade was credited with magical powers, but apple-green was most highly prized as it was believed to confer on the wearer the power of levitation.

The Ruby
This gemstone symbolizes royalty, power and passion. Because of its deep red colour, the ruby was associated with the planet Mars. It was considered by some to be a cure for mental disorders.

The Emerald
A symbol of fertility and rain (because of its green colour), the emerald was associated by the alchemists with wisdom, and by the Christians with faith. In astrology it was linked with the planet Jupiter.

The Diamond
The hardest of all the elements, diamond is associated with permanence and incorruptibility. It also symbolizes the sun and light, and in some early Christian texts stands for Christ.

The Sapphire
The sapphire symbolizes the blue of the heavens, and the heavenly virtues – truth, contemplation and chastity. The alchemists believed it to be a remedy for the bites of venomous animals.

Sun, Moon and Stars

The skies, for ancient peoples, were a screen on which they projected their most profound speculations and spiritual needs. As the prime source of light and heat, the sun combined with rain to bring forth and sustain life. Its active, creative energy was considered to be a male attribute, and because of its high position in the heavens and the clarity of its light, the sun was regarded as all-seeing, and was worshipped as a (mostly masculine) god in a number of civilizations. To the Incas, the sun was a divine ancestor, whose temples were lavishly decorated with gold, the colour with which the sun was closely associated. Even in Christianity the sun was felt to be a worthy symbol of God, standing for the impartiality with which he bestows gifts on all people ("He maketh his sun to rise on the evil and the good"). For Hindus, the sun symbolizes mankind's higher self, and the *Upanishads* (Hindu scriptures) speak of the soul after death ascending by the sun's rays towards the sun itself, "the door to the world, an entrance for the knowing, a bar to the ignorant".

The moon is generally seen as feminine, partly owing to the correspondence of the lunar month with the menstrual cycle. Constantly changing from phase to phase and varying its position in the sky, the moon is capricious in character, but at the same time symbolizes resurrection, immortality and the cyclical nature of all things. It stands for the power of the dark, mysterious side of nature, and the moon goddess was almost universally perceived as the weaver of fate and the controller of destinies, in the same way that she controlled the tides, the weather, rainfall and the seasons.

While the sun and moon symbolized the principal gods, the stars embodied those of lesser importance, whose influence on human fate was more remote. The moon as queen of heaven is often shown haloed with stars to symbolize the obeisance paid to her by the other forces of nature.

The Buddhist Sun Shade
The sun has a fierce, destructive side, which can parch the land, destroying crops and men. In Buddhism, those of high rank were shielded from the sun by parasols, which thus became symbols of the majesty of the Buddhas and bodhisattvas. The parasol also came to represent both the sun (its spokes the rays, its shaft the world axis) and protection from harm.

The Winged Sun Disk
The winged sun disk symbolizes the majesty of the Egyptian sun god Ra, ruler not only of the sun but also of the skies. Recognized as the creator of the world, Ra was revered by the Pharaohs, who considered themselves his sons. Ra resided in the ancient city of Heliopolis where he was worshipped in the form of an obelisk, believed to be a petrified ray of the sun.

The Plough (Big Dipper)
Early astronomers attempted to read meaning into the apparent groupings of stars (the constellations), seeing in them the forms of men, gods and objects. The constellation of the Plough (Big Dipper) was taken to represent the energy that broke up the primal unity of existence into the diverse world of creation.

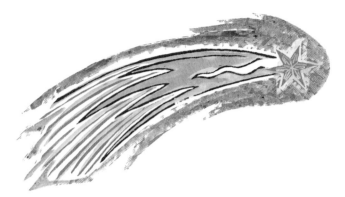

The Dawn
Although the sun has masculine correspondences, dawn is usually seen as female, and in Greek myth was personified as Eos (Aurora), sister of the sun god Helios and moon goddess Selene. She is often depicted rising from the sea or riding across the sky in a horse-drawn chariot. In Buddhism, dawn symbolizes the clear light of the void (ultimate reality), which is seen at the moment of death and, if followed, leads to Nirvana (supreme bliss). In most cultures, the rising sun is a symbol of hope and a new beginning.

The Comet
Comets traditionally have negative connotations. They were seen as manifestations of the wrath of the sun gods or bringers of disaster, war and pestilence. As disruptive forces, they were felt to unsettle the harmony of nature.

The Full Moon
The moon in her open aspect shows the blemishes that are a sign of the decay of all cyclic things. The full moon also echoes the symbolic meanings of the circle, signifying wholeness, completion and achievement.

The Waxing Moon
When waxing, the moon symbolizes creativity, regeneration, female fertility and pregnancy. In European cultures it was believed that sowing seeds at this time resulted in improved germination.

The New Moon
A symbol of ascent from the underworld (the three days of the dark moon). The crescent moon is an attribute of Isis, the Great Mother of the Egyptians, and, in Christian iconography, of the Virgin Mary.

Human and Spiritual Symbols

Most esoteric traditions regard matter and spirit as opposites, which come together only in mankind. The human spirit is considered to be a fragment of the universal energy, the divine principle: it defines mankind's special relationship with God and differentiates the human from the animal. Different cultures see the precise relationship between the human body and spirit very differently, and the way in which these opposites are reconciled is reflected in every aspect of life.

Traditional Christian theology emphasizes the split between spirituality and physicality: the body is seen as no more than a vehicle for the soul (or spirit), which represents the "true" person. The soul is an immortal gift from God, which is joined with the body only temporarily for the duration of a life.

Eastern and occult systems of belief, in contrast, emphasize the interaction between body and spirit. The divide between these opposites is bridged by a number of transitional states (or planes of energy): these intermediate levels are referred to in Hindu writings, such as the *Bhagavadgita*, and correspond to the *sefirah* of the Kabbalistic tree

of life (see page 153). It is on these planes that humanity manifests itself, and the essence of humanity – the soul – is a product of both spirit and matter. It is not surprising, therefore, that Eastern traditions have invested particular parts of the body with special spiritual significance. Certain forms of Hinduism and Buddhism recognize focal points, or chakras (see page 182) within the body, where spiritual and bodily energies interact. Similarly, Chinese acupuncturists can manipulate the life-force (known as *chi*), which is believed to flow through the body along specific pathways (meridians), by inserting needles or applying pressure at certain points. The emphasis on physical preparation in the pursuit of spiritual goals is also evident in Yoga, a system of Indian philosophy.

Much of the symbolism of the body is common to Orient and Occident. For example, the belief that Man was created in the image of God is echoed in depictions of Man as microcosm, and in the construction of Christian churches and Hindu temples, both of which, in their own way, echo the form of the human body (see page 76).

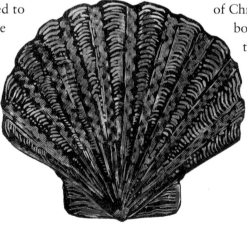

The Scallop Shell
Echoing the shape of the vulva, the scallop shell symbolizes the feminine principle, sexual passion, marriage and fertility.

Creation

The last stage of creation, the making of humanity, was a popular theme in medieval Christian art. Creation myths are perhaps the most important myths in all cultures because they set out mankind's relationship with the gods and the cosmos, and are therefore the foundation stones for all subsequent myths and beliefs.

Sex and Fertility

To the ancients, sexuality was not merely a physical phenomenon, a source of pleasure and a way of reproducing the species. The union of male and female energies in order to produce life was symbolic of all acts of creation, including the fertilization of the land, and even symbolized creation itself. In the Indian cult of Tantra (see page 180), the view of the cosmos was based on the union the male principle (Shiva, often represented by the lingam) with the female (Shakti, symbolized by the yoni, or vulva). By enacting this union in sexual intercourse, the practitioner could achieve a state of blissful enlightenment.

Explicit sexual symbols also appear in the art and myth of pre-Christian European civilizations, though they are linked more to fertility or ribald pleasure than to spiritual enlightenment. For example, in ancient Greece, Priapus, the god of fertility and sexual potency was depicted as a caricature of a man with an enormous phallus: asses, symbols of lecherousness, were sacrificed in his honour. His female counterpart, Baubo, who in Greek myth was a maidservant of the goddess Demeter, was similarly grotesque, appearing as a face on top of an enlarged vulva. A figure of some amusement, she was sometimes depicted astride a pig. In the Celtic world, male deities were commonly shown with an enlarged phallus or triple phallus to emphasize their maleness and ablility to promote fertility.

The natural world is a rich source of fertility symbols: fecund animals, such as the hare, frog, turtle and locust, represent regeneration. The egg, which both carries the potential for new life and resembles the testicles, stands for the continuity of life. In the Christian tradition, the egg is associated with Easter, the time of new growth and of the Resurrection of Christ; and in the mythologies of Japan, India, Polynesia and Scandinavia, it is said that the world itself originated from a primal egg.

The Corn Doll
Fashioned from corn stalks and ears, the corn doll was used as a fertility talisman by women wishing for pregnancy.

Artemis
Artemis (Roman Diana) was goddess of the earth, nature, fertility and childbirth. She symbolizes nature in all her aspects, both kind and cruel.

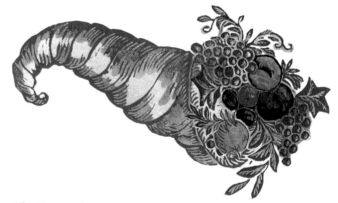

The Cornucopia
The horn of plenty symbolizes the union of male and female, being both phallic and hollow. In Greek myth, the cornucopia belonged to Amalthea (a nymph who took the form of a goat), who cared for the infant Zeus.

The Maypole
The spring fertility rituals of many cultures, from European to native North American, feature dancing around a decorated pole – an obvious phallic symbol representing the annual awakening of nature. At a deeper level, the pole symbolizes the world axis – a support that holds the heavens aloft, and through which the realm of the gods may be reached.

The Wedding Cake
The wedding feast and cake symbolize the link (emphasized by Freudian psychology) between food and sexuality: they also represent the pact of peace (the breaking of bread) between the two families united by the marriage.

The Lingam
A symbol of the masculine creative energy as embodied by the Hindu god Shiva. The lingam stands for regeneration, and, when paired with the yoni (a vulva symbol, usually depicted as a ring at the base of the lingam), for the union of the two sexes.

The Phallic Giant
In much of Europe, as well as the Pacific islands, effigies of giants and nature spirits with erect phalluses were carved in wood and stone, and on hillsides. They represented fertility and the masculine creative power behind the universe.

Body, Youth and Age

For Jaques in Shakespeare's *As You Like It*, human life was divided into seven stages: helplessness ("the infant, mewling and puking in his nurse's arms"); oppression ("the whining schoolboy"); foolishness ("the lover sighing like a furnace"); false pride ("seeking the bubble reputation"); complacency ("the justice, in fair round belly"); ineffectualness ("the lean and slippered pantaloon"); and decay and dissolution ("second childishness and mere oblivion"). Most cultures interpret a person's passage through life less cynically, recognizing three phases of human development – infancy and adolescence, maturity and old age.

The playfulness of childhood is symbolized in Hinduism by Krishna frolicking with the milkmaids, in Christianity by the boy Jesus asking questions of the learned in the temple, and in ancient Egypt by the infant Horus (in the form of Harpocrates, god of silence) listening to the voice of the universe. The achievements and duties of adulthood are embodied in Saint George and in Christ, and in Greek myth by Theseus, who killed the Minotaur to prevent the sacrifice of young lives. The wisdom of old age is symbolically expressed in the Greek god Saturn, who ruled over the universe in the Golden Age, and in Christian depictions of God the father as an old man. In most Eastern traditions, youth and age are seen as two complementary aspects – innocence and wisdom – of the one reality.

In many cultures the human body is a symbol of the indwelling soul. The ancient Egyptians mummified the body so that the departing soul could use it to contact the world of forms. Buddhists, Hindus and medieval Christians revered the physical remains of departed saints. Native North American and Siberian shamans are symbolically torn limb from limb in their inner initiatory journey, only to be revivified into a new wholeness. But the body is symbolically ambivalent. Though sacred, it is also profane, because it shares the lusts of the animal world. In many Western and Middle Eastern traditions, the female body in particular has been a symbol of depravity, because of its power to divert the pure and the strong from their purpose, and the figure of the temptress appears in numerous myths, from the Sirens of ancient Greece to the Teutonic Lorelei (water spirits whose singing lured men to their deaths).

Clothes and Adornments
While nakedness symbolizes innocence and freedom from worldly taint, clothes are more ambivalent. The cloak stands for secrecy and magic powers, while fine robes connote authority and privilege, as well as foolishness and pride. The latter meaning is conveyed by this woodcut from the 18th century, symbolizing vanity and worldliness.

Jewelry
The wearing of jewelry can be seen as an attempt to improve on God's handiwork, and carries negative connotations. Each jewel, however, carries its own, usually positive meaning (see page 118).

A Locket with Hair
Hair, which continues briefly to grow after death, symbolizes a person's life-force and strength: the carrying of a loved one's hair in a locket is a powerful expression of loyalty to their memory.

The Judgment of Paris
At the wedding of the Greek goddess Thetis, Eris (strife) presented a golden apple to be awarded to the fairest woman present. The goddesses Hera, Athene and Aphrodite all claimed the prize: Zeus appointed Paris, the son of Priam (king of Troy), as judge in the beauty contest. Paris chose Aphrodite, who promised to reward him with the love of any woman he chose, and described the beauty of Helen, the wife of the king of Sparta. Paris abducted Helen, and brought her back to Troy, an action which precipitated the Trojan war, in which he was killed. The myth conveys the idea that physical beauty, though alluring, can ultimately be destructive.

The Hand
The right hand is usually associated with rectitude and the left with deviousness. Hand gestures carry specific meanings: for example, the thumbs-up sign originally stood for virility. Hindus and Buddhists use a system of more than five hundred gestures, or *mudras*, in ritual and dance.

The Foot and Footprint
Feet represent stability and freedom. It was believed that they could draw energy from the ground. Indentations in rocks were seen as the footprints of the gods. Buddha's footprints (above) show symbols of divinity: by following in his footsteps, mankind may reach enlightenment.

The Heart
The heart is the basic symbol for sincerity, love and compassion, and also represents the centre of things. Pierced by an arrow, and surmounted by a cross or crowned with thorns, it is a symbol of the saints, while the heart with wings or on the bared breast denotes Christ.

The Skeleton
The skeleton usually represents mortality and the vanity of human wishes, but can also stand for the ascetic's renounciation of physical comforts. In alchemical symbolism, the skeleton is equated with the *nigredo* (see page 149), the stage of death before resurrection.

Father Time
A symbol of the impermanence of human endeavour, Father Time is associated with Cronos, the Greek god of agriculture, from whom he acquired the attribute of the sickle. He is also commonly depicted carrying an hourglass.

Good and Evil

Good and evil, antagonistic forces at large in the universe, are characteristically represented by irreconcilable opposites – beauty versus ugliness, courage versus cowardice, and so on. In Christian symbolism, few tread the straight and narrow path that leads to eternal life, the majority following the broad road to damnation. Good and evil are embodied in the Holy Trinity and Satan, the father of lies (who is sometimes shown with three faces as a way of making the comparison between the two more explicit). In most cultures, the long-term rewards of goodness are symbolized as treasures worth pursuing, while the punishments attendant upon evil are truly horrifying. The Eastern idea of karma is less final in its judgment, allowing unlimited opportunities for redemption. Every human action is a cause that carries an equivalent effect, in this life, in the after-life, or in another incarnation in this world. There is no escaping this law, as it is as much a part of the natural order as old age or gravity.

However, many of the world's great esoteric traditions reject the idea of good and evil as opposites and teach that every action contains elements of both. For example, by cultivating the land a person might disturb the balance of nature, or by saving a life might preserve someone who will go on to destroy others. Conversely, a doctor might inflict pain to treat a wound, or a soldier take one life in order to save hundreds. Everyday existence depends upon the death of plants and animals, without which there can be no life. Thus, good and evil are not in conflict, and indeed depend on one another. This notion is clearly expressed in the Tai Chi symbol below.

The Tai Chi (Yin Yang)
This ancient Eastern symbol represents balance between the opposing forces necessary to produce the world of forms. Each carries within it the seed of the other. Male and female, right and left, and good and evil, depend on their opposites for their own expression.

The Demon
The Greek word *daimon* (later *daemon*) originally meant god, before degenerating to represent first a nature spirit, and then an imp of hell. The demon now symbolizes an active force for evil, which can corrupt human behaviour in the service of its master, Satan.

The Archangel
Appearing primarily in Western religions, archangels represent aspects of the divine energy. In Christianity, the archangels Michael, Raphael, Uriel and Gabriel carry a sword, a pilgrim's staff, a book and a lily respectively, symbolizing divine judgment, protection, wisdom and mercy.

The Monk
Followers of the monastic life symbolize piety, austerity and withdrawal from the world into a life dedicated to spiritual progress. The monk also stands for healing (hospital care was first offered in monasteries), refuge for travellers, scholarship and disciplined work.

Haloes, Masks and Shadows

The halo or nimbus is best known from its appearances in Christian iconography from the 2nd century onward, but was used as a sign of divinity or sainthood much earlier, featuring in ancient Greek and Eastern art. It may represent the aura, the field of energy believed by some to surround the human body; or it may stand for the sun, and therefore for the divine radiance emanating from the individual.

Negatively related to the halo is the shadow, the aspect of mankind that interrupts the flow of light from heaven to earth. It is a symbol of our material nature, of the density of form as opposed to the transparency of spirit. The mask can stand for the artificial, public face that conceals a person's true nature – that is, for role rather than reality. However, in shamanism and Tibetan Buddhism, it is believed that the mask can help an individual to go beyond role and relinquish the ego, allowing the spirits of helpful animals or even gods to enter and work through him or her.

The Halo
A symbol of divine radiance, the wisdom of the gods and the emanation of life-force from the head. In Christian art, the halo is usually round, and white or golden in colour. In the Eastern Orthodox Church, Christ's halo often has a cross within it.

The Shadow
The shadow is the sign of materiality, and it was thought that spirits could be recognized by their lack of a shadow. In Jungian terms, the shadow is the repressed or imperfectly acknowledged part of oneself.

Variations on the Halo
In some traditions, a square or hexagonal halo indicates that the "wearer" is still alive, while a round halo denotes a dead saint. The halo of God the Father is often triangular or diamond-shaped.

The Mandorla
The oval mandorla (the Italian word for "almond") is a variant of the halo that surrounds the whole body of a holy person. It symbolizes power as well as spirituality and often appears around the body of Christ in paintings depicting the Ascension.

The Mask

Masks suggest concealment or transformation. They were used to put the wearer in closer touch with deities, spirits and the instinctual wisdom of animals. In the East, the mask is taken as a symbol of the great illusion of existence: the world itself is *maya*, the mask of God. In Greek theatre and in Japanese Noh plays, masks signal the individual qualities of the characters concerned, and allow the audience to identify more closely with them by depersonalizing the actors.

Gods and Goddesses

Early written records, such as the Hindu *Rig Vedas* (some of which date from around 1,000BC), indicate that the ancients had a sophisticated appreciation of the energy forces that went to create and sustain life. However, the origin of these forces was beyond description or comprehension, so it was natural for people to present a rationalized, symbolic picture of ultimate realities. In psychological terms, the early peoples projected outward the archetype (see page 13) of higher powers, and thus emerged the concept of the gods – beings graced with all the qualities to which people aspired in their own lives. In many cultures, the gods proliferated, each symbolizing a particular aspect of nature (thunder, the sea, fire, war) or a particular human attribute (compassion, beauty, wisdom). In the most sophisticated forms of religion the individual gods were subservient to, or components of, an ultimate, higher power variously symbolized as a sun or sky god or, less concretely, as infinite potential or emptiness.

This is not to reduce the gods to mere figments of mankind's fertile imagination. Arguably, the power that created and sustained the universe does indeed reveal itself to humanity in symbolic forms adjusted to mankind's ability to comprehend, and the gods are therefore a synthesis of divine energy and the limitations of human thought.

Jung believed that the human psyche has a "natural religious function", a pressing need to give conscious expression to unconscious archetypes. This desire – equal in potency to the instincts of sexuality and aggression – may explain the vast energies channelled into building temples and cathedrals, fighting religious wars, and converting members of other faiths. Jung argued that attempts to stifle these urges (especially later in life when youthful ambitions no longer provide sufficient motivation) could lead to psychic instability or breakdown.

God the Father
In Christian art, which reflects the attitudes of predominantly patriarchal societies, God is usually depicted as a wise father figure with a long white beard (a symbol of dignity). Before the 15th century, such images were rare, and paintings of Biblical events usually showed God in the form of Christ, recognizable by a cruciform halo. Islam forbids direct representations of Allah, to avoid misconceptions that may ultimately impede belief.

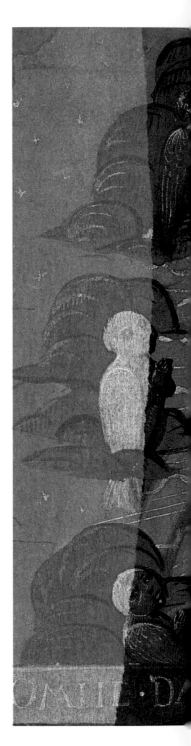

A·OPTIMVM·DE·SVRSV·ES

The Tetragrammaton
The name of God revealed to Moses as four Hebrew letters YHWH is known as the tetragrammaton. This sacred word is thought to be derived from God's statement in Exodus: "I am that I am."

Kuan Yin
A Chinese symbol of godly purity and wisdom. Buddhists see Kuan Yin as the female form of Avalokiteshvara, the thousand-armed bodhisattva who represents infinite compassion.

Durga
In Hindu symbology, male and female creative energies are always held in balance. Thus, each of the gods has a consort, equal in importance to himself. Durga, the consort of Shiva, is the divine mother of the universe, the destroyer of evil (in which role she is sometimes identified with the terrifying Kali), and the symbol of insight, discrimination, devotion and bliss. She is often represented as ten-armed (a symbol of majesty and strength) and riding a lion (spiritual power).

Quetzalcoatl
This is the Plumed Serpent, the Aztec supreme god of the wind and the west. Often associated by Europeans with human sacrifice, Quetzalcoatl was in fact a symbol of gentleness, wisdom and law-making: he was responsible for conquering the devouring earth-serpent and rendering the world habitable. Human sacrifices were offered not to Quetzalcoatl himself but to appease the earth serpent, which still longed for blood.

Saturn

The Roman god of seed, agriculture and plenty (equated with the Greek god Cronos), Saturn ruled the earth in the Golden Age – the mythical first, paradisal epoch after creation. His festival, Saturnalia, a celebration of the winter solstice, was a time of freedom and indulgence, and is thought to be the origin of the Western Christmas celebrations.

Shiva

One of the three principal Hindu deities, and lord of the cosmic dance, Shiva destroys so that life can be renewed. In one of his four hands he carries the flame that consumes and in another the rattle whose sound calls forth creation. His third hand is held out in a gesture of fearlessness, while his fourth points to the dwarf of ignorance under his feet.

Witches, Priests and Wizards

Respected or reviled, those people privy to the inner secrets of true wisdom have always held a special place in society. The idea of witchcraft is ancient and widespread, occurring in the traditions of Europe, Africa and North America, and is thought by anthropologists to have a well-defined social purpose. Possessed by supposedly disruptive or evil spirits, the witch is in fact a scapegoat upon whom calamities and social conflicts can be blamed. With the advent of Christianity, witches were seen as the devil's instruments, and the Biblical invocation to "not permit a sorceress to live" was taken literally as late as 1692, when nineteen convicted witches were hanged in the Massachusetts Bay Colony of Salem. Witches were often characterized as seductresses or cannibals, or depicted as owls, cats and toads in the belief that they could physically transform themselves into these creatures of the night.

In contrast to the witch, the priest has usually symbolized the authorized use of inner wisdom, administering the religion practised or approved by community leaders. In ancient Egyptian and some South American cultures, the priests were also the kings, occupying their temporal position by virtue of their spiritual powers. In few cultures was the priesthood exclusively male: feminine energy was seen to be symbolic of the secret, hidden side of nature, and in most Mediterranean societies women were considered to be possessed of greater spiritual power than men. This belief was expressed through the widespread worship of female deities such as Isis and Artemis.

Wizards have traditionally occupied a role somewhere between that of witches and priests, being capable of serving either good or evil. Essentially workers of ritual magic, in their most exalted form they were concerned with raising their consciousness toward communion with the divine, and with gaining control over the powers of nature.

The Wizard
Wizards symbolize magical powers for good (wizards of the right-hand path) or ill (left-hand path), but can also represent the wisdom that comes with age, and the solitary, scholarly life.

The Witch
Symbolizing destruction and dark powers, the witch is usually, but not always, depicted as a woman. In the West, she is characteristically a hag on a broomstick, but in Africa she is fat from eating human flesh and red-eyed from her nocturnal pursuits.

Heaven and Hell

For the ancients, the sky was the natural abode of the gods, who controlled sunlight, rain and the other natural forces upon which life depended. Often the gods were believed to live on a solid dome (or firmament) above the earth, from which they observed and judged the activities of mortals. The heavens, or heaven (the two words are similar in most languages), were thus the obvious place of reward for a good life. And as the opposite of heaven, hell – a dark subterranean world – came to symbolize the place of punishment and retribution.

Descriptions of heaven vary greatly between cultures. In many Western interpretations, heaven is merely a distillation of earthly pleasures. Christian artists often depicted heaven as a beautiful garden or orchard, and the Norse heaven of Valhalla was a place of constant feasting and drinking. In the Inca and ancient Egyptian traditions, heaven had a more spiritual dimension, being a place of inner peace and liberation from carnal desires. Visions of hell are similarly diverse. Christian art saw hell as the abode of the Devil guarded by the three-headed dog Cerberus (borrowed from Greek mythology) and carried grave warnings of the infernal retribution for specific sins: fornicators, for example, were punished by having their genitals eaten by insects and toads. In the Islamic tradition, the bodies of sinners are enlarged in order to aggravate their suffering in hell. The ancient Greeks believed that Hades, the underworld, consisted of three realms: the Plain of Asphodel, a limbo world where souls were destined to wander aimlessly; the Elysian Plain, which was the destination of the fortunate few; and Tartarus, where the wicked were punished.

Eastern religions generally place more emphasis on rebirth, and final release from the cycle of becoming, than on finite concepts such as heaven and hell. For example, in Buddhism heaven and hell are seen as places where one works off the merits or demerits accrued in this life before returning once more to the world of incarnation.

Paradise
Paradise is seen as a place of peace, light, and beauty, echoing the primordial perfection of nature. It sometimes represents heaven itself and sometimes a stage on the road toward it. It may be depicted as a garden or, in the Christian tradition, as the New Jerusalem.

Tsitigarbharaja
The concept of eternal hell is at odds with Buddhist teachings. Buddhism embodies enduring love and compassion in Tsitigarbharaja, the bodhisattva who descends into hell in order to teach and rescue those suffering there.

Jacob's Ladder
In Genesis, Jacob dreams of angels ascending and descending a ladder between heaven and earth. The ladder indicates that mankind can ascend to heaven and the divine can descend to earth, but also implies that the link between the two is unstable.

The Japanese Hell
In Japanese visions of hell, sinners are judged by Emma-o, lord of the underworld, who is usually depicted holding his staff of office. After judgment, sinners are consigned to one of sixteen regions of fire or ice, and can be saved only by the prayers of the living.

The Flaming Sword
When Adam and Eve were expelled from Eden, God placed "a flaming sword that turned every way" to the east of the garden. It symbolizes the sacrifice that must now be made by those wishing to re-enter the garden – the surrender of the ego that believes itself separate from God.

Nirvana
The supreme goal of the Buddhists, Nirvana is beyond description: it is ultimate tranquillity, the release from all the limitations of existence, and is symbolized in only the most abstract form.

Charon and Styx
Death has always been symbolized as a journey – the flight of the soul to the court of Osiris, the sea crossing to the Isles of the Blessed, the ride with the Valkyries to Valhalla. For the Greeks, the journey was across the River Styx, ferried by Charon the ghostly boatman. To pay for this dark passage the dead were buried with coins in their mouths.

Symbol Systems

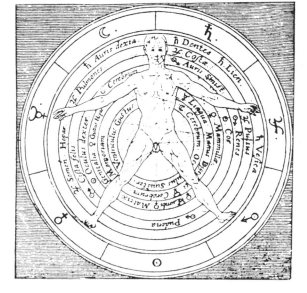

 In the extraordinary richness and complexity of symbol systems such as the Tarot, Astrology and the Kabbalah, we see human creativity at full stretch. However, we can also detect something much deeper than this. The fascination of symbol systems is that they resonate with fundamental aspects of our own nature, speaking to us of shared wisdom whose truths we recognize but can never quite put into words. It seems probable that symbols systems were visualized by people who were in closer contact with profound realities than we are today.

A symbol system is nothing less than a symbolic map of reality. It represents the topography of the mental and emotional realm that reveals itself to the inner eye. And just as a city cannot be properly appreciated unless we allow ourselves the time and space to study it in its every detail, so too a symbol system can only reveal its full meaning if we acquaint ourselves with all its aspects. Each symbol in the system has meaning not only in its own right, but also in relationship to the other symbols. As with a piece of complex orchestral music, the whole is much more than the sum of its individual parts.

The Greco-Armenian mystic and philosopher, George Ivanovitch Gurdjieff (1872–1949), suggested that we are like people living in beautiful houses who never venture out of the basement. The mind is indeed analagous to a beautiful house, and unless we explore those parts of it that lie outside everyday thinking then, in a very real sense, we remain strangers to ourselves. The study of a symbol system can provide a key to a better understanding of our own minds and enable us to live more fully within them.

Those wishing to orientate themselves on the spiritual map that a symbol system provides usually find that one system exerts a greater pull than the rest. In part, this is the result of cultural factors, but individual temperament also plays a role. To someone who is artistic, or has a highly developed visual sense, a system that uses pictures (such as the Tarot) may appeal the most. A person for whom the body is paramount over the intellect may lean toward a system focused upon the body's energy centres (such as the Eastern yogic system). In addition, certain symbol systems make greater demands on their students than others. For example, initiation into some of the occult systems is a lengthy process, in which the inner truths that magical symbols represent are revealed piecemeal to the student, to protect him or her from the psychological damage that a sudden release of psychic energy could cause. Similarly, alchemical symbols are deliberately cryptic in order to test the resolve and motivation of the seeker.

A New Synthesis

All the great symbol systems attempt to reflect paradoxical truths about the ultimate reality in terms far removed from the commonsensical language of every day. They communicate in a specialized idiom of their own, because plain language is inadequate to penetrate below the surface of things, however efficient it may be for mundane concerns. Worn thin by overuse, our common tongue cannot illuminate the deepest realities. Rational logic, similarly, is incapable of unveiling for us the most important kinds of knowledge. In the modern age, we must learn to recapture instinctive, pre-scientific truths – the ancient beliefs that spiritual symbol systems have handed on to us.

Patient study of a chosen system will refresh our minds not least by suggesting an alternative way of looking at the world. Of course, it would be folly to turn our back on the discoveries of science. But in the 1990s science is becoming less certain of itself, and with the development of new fields such as quantum mechanics we are beginning to regain the old sense of mystery. Quantum theory argues that we can know the position of a particle, and we can know its momentum, but we cannot know both: our viewpoint limits understanding. The theories of Einstein, who astounded us by insisting that space is curved, and was able to prove it, now seem perfectly orthodox, even quaint, to those versed in the modern mysteries of science.

The world is moving toward a synthesis of disciplines, one science informing another, until the traditional distinctions of knowledge become dissolved. We must hope that past and present wisdom, material and spiritual disciplines, will support each other in the same way, the past throwing a deep-reaching spiritual light upon the present – as it does already for many of those who have unravelled the complexities of traditional symbolism and deciphered the hidden meanings contained therein.

Vishnu as Macrocosm

Depictions of Man as macrocosm occur in numerous symbol systems. In this Indian painting, the best-loved and most human of Vishnu's avatars, Krishna, is shown as a symbol of the world, containing men, animals and the heavens in his body. Four-armed Krishna holds his attributes – the discus, conch, lotus flower and club.

Occult Systems

The word "occult", which arouses suspicion in many minds, means merely "hidden". An occult system is a system of wisdom which its practitioners feel must be kept secret. The common thread that unites the many different systems of occult belief is their use of symbolic devices to bring about a profound change in consciousness, which allows the adept to discover truths about his or her own nature, and about reality itself.

The origins of Western occultism can be traced back to the texts of the *Hermetica*, which date from the 1st–3rd century AD. These works take the form of dialogues between deities, often including the Greek god Hermes Trismegistus. They enshrine a number of concepts that emerge later in the history of the occult, such as the duality of matter and spirit, and the idea that salvation can be achieved through knowledge rather than faith. The *Hermetica* views mankind as an immortal spirit trapped in a mortal body, from which we are able to achieve liberation, and thus union with God, by understanding his own true nature. Also recorded in these texts is an account of how the ancients brought their gods to life from statues by assembling the emblems of the gods around the statues and intoning secret words revealed to them by the deities concerned.

The *grimoires*, the magical "recipe books" of the Middle Ages (the most famous of which is the *Key of Solomon*), set out a system in which self-knowledge, and therefore full spiritual evolution, could be attained by the use of symbols to invoke spirits. Having put on

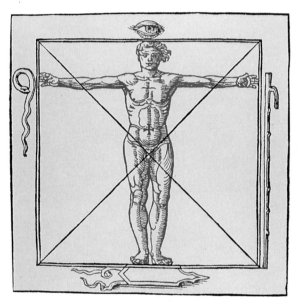

his vestments and assembled his magical weapons, the practitioner drew on the ground a complex symbol (a kind of Western mandala) which represented his body, mind and soul, and alongside it a second triangular shape. The spirit was then summoned into the triangle and confronted by the magician: if he failed to subdue it, the spirit would enter the mandala and destroy him. This process may be interpreted in a psycho-spiritual context, with the spirits representing facets of the magician himself, which must be conquered and understood in order to develop a fully integrated personality.

Later occult systems, such as the Hermetic Order of the Golden Dawn (founded in London in 1887), were strongly influenced by the theories of Eliphas Lévi (see opposite). In common with many other systems, there were seven levels of initiation – Neophyte, Zelator, Theoricus, Practicus, Philosophus, Adeptus Minor, and Adeptus Major. A practitioner at the highest level had three tasks – divination, evocation and invocation. In each of these tasks, symbolism played an essential part. When practising divination, the adept would use symbolic systems such as the Tarot or I Ching. When practising evocation, he would surround himself with symbols of the god (or the part of his own consciousness) with which he wished to make contact. Over a period of days these symbols would put the adept in an appropriate state of consciousness. At the right moment, through appropriate rituals, he would invoke the deity and whatever powers he possessed.

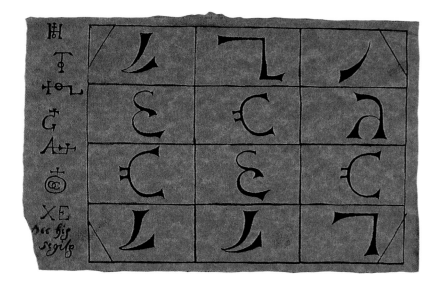

Magical Script (left)
The English occultist and mathematician John Dee (who served as astrologer in the court of Elizabeth I) attempted to relate magical symbols to Pythagorean geometry and mathematical proportions. The philosophy behind his magical script was later adopted by a number of secret fraternities.

Magical Diagram (opposite page)
In this diagram from Cornelius Agrippa's *De Occulta Philosophia*, a 16th-century occult text, Man is surrounded by four magical symbols – the eye, staff, snake and shield.

The Rosy Cross
The occult system of Rosicrucianism emerged in 17th-century Germany with the publication of a pamphlet entitled *The Fama and Fraternity of the Meritorious Order of the Rosy Cross*. Its alleged author, the possibly fictitious German nobleman Christian Rosycross, is held to have founded a mystical fraternity, whose occult practices and beliefs were closely associated with Alchemy and the Kabbalah. The symbol with which Rosicrucianism is most closely associated is the rose placed between the arms of a cross, representing the unfolding of spiritual realities within. The arms of the cross bear the four Hebraic letters of the Tetragrammaton (see page 133).

The Magic of Eliphas Lévi
Born in 1810, Eliphas Lévi turned his back on a calling to the priesthood and spent years practising ritual magic. One of the greatest theoreticians of the occult, Lévi formulated three fundamental and highly influential occult doctrines. *The Law of Correspondence* stated that man was a "little universe" of which every part corresponded exactly with a part of the greater universe. *The Dogma of High Magic* stated that the human will was capable of achieving anything, if properly trained and focused. *The Astral Light* was held by Lévi to be an invisible force permeating the universe. Shown in this engraving from Lévi's *Transcendental Magic* are the magician's tools – lamp, rod, dagger and sword.

Alchemy

Alchemy is commonly viewed as a pseudo-science concerned with the transformation of base metals into gold: its status is that of a curiosity, notable mainly for the contributions of its practitioners to the emerging discipline of chemistry. This misconception is understandable given the shroud of secrecy deliberately drawn over the true goal of alchemy – the attainment of enlightenment. At the most esoteric level, the base metal of the alchemist was symbolic of the unredeemed self, while the gold, with its incorruptible nature and capacity to shine steadily, was symbolic of the transformed spiritual self. The intention was to turn the dross of everyday thought and experience into a pure, spiritual state.

MONS PHILOSOPHORVM

Great Work – had interdependent physical and spiritual dimensions.

Alchemy is thought to have originated in ancient Egypt, and to have been part of the esoteric wisdom of the Greeks, Arabs, Indians and Chinese. The first alchemical text to appear in Western Europe was the 12th-century translation into Latin by an Englishman, Robert of Chester, of the Arabic *Book of the Composition of Alchemy*. The theory underlying alchemical practice derives from the ancient world-view, in which the whole of reality, including mankind, is created from a non-physical *materia prima* (first matter) – the universal magical element – that takes form as the elements earth, fire, air and water. Because these elements can be transformed into one another, it is apparent that all material things are based upon the principle of change. According to this world-view, it was possible to transform a substance back into the *materia prima*, and conversely the *materia prima* could be returned to the world in a different form.

The symbolism of alchemical transformation was used to disguise what the powerful medieval European Church condemned as an heretical practice, since it was based upon the belief that the individual could raise himself or herself toward salvation without the agency of established religion. But alchemy was more than just a symbol of inner transformation: it provided the means by which this could be achieved. Alchemists aimed to transmute the base material into the "philosopher's stone", also known as the Elixir or Tincture. Turning base metals into gold was proof of its power, but the elixir was an aim in itself, an essence rather than merely an agent. The journey to enlightenment – known to alchemists as the

The practice of alchemy is laid out in medieval texts so obscure and loaded with symbolism as to be nearly incomprehensible. Some scholars argue that in defying conventional logic, these texts test the resolve of the seeker, who must rely on inspiration and intuition to guide him on the path to enlightenment. More cynical commentators hold that the tortuous texts merely conceal a fraud. However, it is clear that the alchemist begins the Great Work with the *materia prima* which it

Alchemical Keys
This engraving – one of a series of twelve 17th-century pictorial "keys" of the alchemist – contains symbols that refer to stages in the alchemical process. The sun and moon are the male and female elements of alchemy respectively; the two roses, red and white, symbolize the Red King and White Queen. Between them is the symbol of Mercury, the transforming agent of the alchemical process, which is released from the *materia prima*, transformed and brought to perfection through the alchemist's operations. Fire, an external force in alchemy, is here shown burning in a wooden brazier; alchemical texts often refer to a cool fire, which heats the contents of the alchemist's vessel gently, like a chicken incubating her eggs. The lion and snake are both symbols of raw, unrefined matter.

The Ascent to Enlightenment (opposite page)
The Great Work of the alchemists is here depicted as the ascent of a mountain, the *Mons Philosophorum*. At its summit is a pearl, a symbol of the rainbow colours into which the *nigredo* is transformed at the end of the first stage of the Great Work (see page 149).

The Philosopher's Stone
In this image from the *Mutus Liber*, or "Silent Book", a 17th-century pictorial book, the philosopher's stone is shown (below) in the Athanor (alchemists' furnace), while its archetype is personified as Mercury (above) in the hands of the angels. The image emphasizes that the physical operations of alchemy mirror a spiritual reality, a belief summarized in the words of the French alchemist Pierre-Jean Fabre: "Alchemy is not merely an art or science to teach metallic transmutation, so much as a true and solid science that teaches how to know the centre of all things, which in the divine language is called the Spirit of Life."

is claimed one must mine for oneself, and which takes the form of a "stone" (not to be confused with the philosopher's stone itself). This stone, whose exact nature is nowhere revealed, is pulverized and mixed with a "first agent", enigmatically described as "dry water" or as "fire without flame", which some alchemists suggest is prepared by a secret process from cream of tartar. The resulting amalgam of these two substances is moistened with spring dew and placed in a sealed vessel or "philosopher's egg", and heated at a constant temperature over a long period.

During incubation, the two principles within the *materia prima*, usually referred to symbolically as "sulphur" (red, male, solar, hot energy) and "mercury" (white, female, lunar, cold energy) are said to fight venomously, each eventually slaying the other and producing a black putrefaction, the *nigredo*, the "black of blacks". This completes the first stage of the Great Work. In the second stage, the blackness becomes overlaid with rainbow colours (sometimes depicted as a peacock tail or pearl), which are in turn covered by a whiteness, the *albedo*. At this point, the two principles of the *materia prima* reappear in a new form, as the "red king" (Sulphur of the Wise) emerges from the womb of the "white queen" (mercury, or the White Rose). The King and Queen are united in the fire of love, and from their union comes perfection, the philosopher's stone, the catalyst capable of transmuting base metals into gold and the key to enlightenment.

For the alchemist, correct motivation was essential in undertaking the Great Work. The quest of those who concentrated merely on the chemical processes was doomed to fail. If the seeker was driven by greed, then, as one alchemical text puts it, he would "reap but smoke". Instead, he should be motivated "to know nature and its operations, and make use of this knowledge ... to reach the Creator".

The original "stone", which the seeker must mine for himself, symbolizes the deep inner longing to find our true spiritual nature, known to alchemists as the "active principle". The "first agent" stands for the "passive principle", the indwelling energy of which most of us are unaware as we travel through life, but which carries the potential for spiritual growth. Once contact is made between the active and passive principles within the "furnace" of deep meditation, a struggle ensues as the active principle, used to obtaining what it wants through the exercise of the will, finds that the passive principle cannot be vanquished in this way. There follows the dark night of the soul of which mystics speak, in which both active and passive principles seem to have been annihilated and the individual feels utterly forsaken. Out of this despair, however, arises the rainbow revelation that love and not force is required, and this is followed by the union of the two principles, the red king and the white queen, whose progeny is born of water and the spirit.

What were the actual spiritual practices behind this symbolic process? Meditating upon the alchemical symbols themselves, in a progression through each of the stages, was certainly involved. But a Chinese alchemical text, *The Secret of the Golden Flower*, gives us further clues. It tells us how, through meditation, physical energy can be visualized as gathering and concentrating in the lower body, in the "place of power" below the navel, where it generates immense heat and then (symbolically) passes "the boiling point [and] mounts upwards like flying snow ... to the summit of the Creative".

Perhaps, for all their quaint and obscure language, the alchemists (or a few among them) did indeed effect the union of the red king and the white queen, and raised the base metal of the physical being into the pure gold of the greater spiritual self.

The Androgyne

The primal elements of sulphur (that which burns) and mercury (that which is volatile) are embodied in the androgyne or hermaphrodite. The union of these opposite principles is the purpose of alchemy and of human endeavour itself. The androgyne wears the crown of perfection. It stands on a dragon – a serpent with bird's feet – symbolizing its dominion over the forces of land, sea and air. The four heads of the dragon represent the four elements – fire, air, water and earth.

The Lion Eating the Sun
Alchemy is connected with numerous different systems of thought. At one time or another, the art has been practised in Northern Europe, Greece, India, China and the Middle East. It is not surprising, therefore, that alchemical symbols have numerous, sometimes conflicting interpretations. For example, the green lion (above), which represents matter in a primordial state, can be said to be devouring the male principle, or liberating the sulphur of the wise (both of which may be symbolized by the sun).

Alchemy and Christianity
Many alchemists were good Christians, but preferred to seek knowledge through direct experience rather than blind faith. Men such as Thomas Aquinas and Isaac Newton considered alchemy to be a complement to established philosophy and religion. The above detail from the "Ripley Scroll" shows the bird of Hermes (Mercury) drenched in sacred dew. The Ripley scroll was designed by Sir George Ripley, a devout English aristocrat, who was a Canon in the Augustinian priory at Bridlington, Yorkshire.

The King and Queen
In this woodcut from the 1550 edition of the *Rosarium Philosophorum*, the King and Queen, symbolic of the male (solar) and female (lunar) principles, are pictured in sexual congress in the archetypal "sea" of the spirit. In Jungian psychology, the King, Queen and other alchemical symbols are believed to correspond to the universal archetypes of the unconscious (see page 13).

The Kabbalah

The Kabbalah is an extraordinary system of theoretical and practical wisdom designed to provide its students not only with a path of mental and spiritual growth, but also with a symbolic map of creation itself. Rooted in 3rd-century mysticism, the Kabbalah developed in an essentially Hebrew tradition, and the earliest known Kabbalistic text, the *Sefer Yetzira*, appeared some time between the 3rd and 6th centuries. The powerful appeal of the system led to its incorporation into certain aspects of Christian thinking in the 15th century. The Italian scholar Giovanni Pico della Mirandola argued that "no science can better convince us of the divinity of Jesus Christ than magic and the Kabbalah". Other Christian writers felt that the Kabbalah contained a revelation to mankind, now lost, by means of which it was possible to comprehend fully the classical Greek teachings of Pythagoras, Plato and the Orphics.

Essentially, the Kabbalah is an esoteric teaching centred on a system of symbols, which are held to reflect the mystery of God and the universe, and for which the Kabbalist must find the key. At the theoretical level, these keys allow him (the Kaballist has traditionally been male) to understand the spiritual dimensions of the universe, while at the practical level they allow him to use the powers associated with these

God the Creator
In this Christian interpretation of the Kabbalah, God is shown setting out the laws that govern the universe. The shape of the Creator's throne mirrors that of the macrocosm: the throne cover is a model of the heavens, the back a representation of the planetary spheres.

dimensions for magical purposes (that is for the processes of physical, psychological or spiritual transformation). The keys to the Kabbalah lie hidden in the meaning of the divine revelations which make up the holy scriptures: just as God is hidden, so too are the inner secrets of his divine message. These secrets may be revealed by decoding the scriptures through a system of numerical equivalences or *gematria,* in which each letter of the Hebrew alphabet has a number associated with it, or can be permutated or abbreviated in certain ways. For example, the brass serpent constructed by Moses and set on a pole so that "if a serpent had bitten any man, when he beheld the serpent of brass he lived" (Numbers 21:9) is converted through *gematria* to the number 358, which is also the numerical equivalent of the word "Messiah". Thus, the brass serpent is held to be a prophecy of the coming of the Messiah, who will save all those bitten by the longing for spiritual truth. This led Christian Kabbalists to adopt the symbol of the serpent draped over the cross to represent Christ.

So extensive are the possibilities for *gematria* that an understanding of Hebrew is neccessary in order to study the Kabbalah. In the past, Kabbalists insisted on a number of further stringent conditions before accepting students: the candidates had to lead morally pure lives, have great powers of concentration and be completely dedicated to the task. For this reason, the Kabbalah is known to most people only in its most accessible form – the *sefiroth*, or tree of life (right). But despite its apparent simplicity, the sefiroth is itself a powerful and all-encompassing symbol.

In its fundamental interpretation, the sefiroth explains creation. The reason for existence is held to be that God wished to behold himself: to accomplish this, he withdrew his presence – the Absolute All – from one place so that he could "gaze upon his own face". In the act of calling the universe into being, God revealed ten of his attributes, each of which is represented in the sefiroth by a *sefirah*. The sefirah are linked together in a set of precise relationships: the path begins at Keter (the crown) which denotes all that was, is and will be, and leads eventually to Malkhut (the kingdom) which corresponds to the presence of God in matter. The direction of the path from Keter to Malkhut, through the attributes of wisdom, understanding, mercy, judgment, beauty, eternity, reverberation and foundation, is governed by the three Divine Principles of Will, Mercy and Justice. In most visualizations of the sefiroth, the path takes the form of a zigzag or lightning flash as the three divine principles, which are associated with balance (Will), expansion (Mercy) and constraint (Justice), operate in turn.

Although all the laws relating to being and creation are embedded within the sefiroth, they exist as unrealized plans. In order to account for the many manifestations of God, the Kabbalah contains the concept of the Four Worlds or cosmic cycles, each of which has its own Tree of Life. The Four Worlds – Manifestation, Creation, Formation and Action – can be seen as the different aspects of God through which the universe was brought into being. They refer also to the hierarchy of the Worlds revealed to the 6th-century prophet

The Kabbalistic Tree
The diagram of the sefiroth was first published in the Middle Ages, and there have since been many variations on its basic struture. In this 20th-century version from a notebook of the Order of the Golden Cross (a magical fraternity), the ten sefirah are linked together by twenty-two pathways – the number of elemental letters in the Hebrew alphabet. One letter is thus assigned to each pathway, and together with the ten sefirah themselves, this yields thirty-two avenues of wisdom. The nature of each connecting pathway is determined both by the letter associated with it and by the two sefirah that it links together. Superimposed on the sefiroth in this occult version is the Great Serpent, which is linked with Kundalini energy (see page 182).

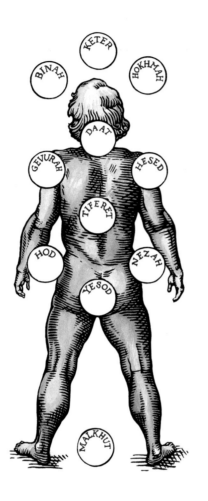

Adam Kadmon
In Kabbalistic belief, primordial Man, known as Adam Kadmon, was called forth in the form of the sefiroth. In this human form, endowed with will, intellect, emotion, and a capacity to be conscious of his divine creator, Adam Kadmon was a reflection of God and an expression of the Divine Attributes, containing everything needed to allow God to gaze upon His own reflection. He is usually shown from behind, just as, in the Old Testament, Moses saw the divine image from behind; however, later Kabbalists used Adam's face as a metaphor of the mercy through which Divine radiance emanated. Adam Kadmon is the progenitor of the Adam of Genesis, through whom God's image was brought into the World of Formation (the Garden of Eden).

Ezekiel who, in a vision, saw the likeness of the glory of God (Manifestation) on a throne (Creation), riding in a chariot (Formation) above the world (Action). Each world possesses all the characteristics of the one above, and so is more complex and subject to more laws. The Four Worlds are usually depicted as four interlocking sefiroth – the extended tree of life.

The patterns and relationships enshrined in the sefiroth are fundamental to being and can therefore be applied to all areas of knowledge and endeavour. Properly used and understood, the sefiroth is a blueprint from which all phenomena – from cosmic forces to human relationships, from the ascent of the soul toward God to the fate of world economies – can be explained and ultimately controlled.

The Kabbalah is essentially an oral tradition, and the initiate is usually guided by an experienced mentor who stands in for the student's imperfectly developed consciousness and steers him away from the dangers inherent in mystical experience. The initiate usually starts by studying the ten sefirah, ascending the tree towards full enlightenment. Each sefirah represents an aspect of the self that must be fully developed before the student can proceed to the stages that lie beyond. For example, unless he has come properly to terms with Malkuth, the world of the body and its energies, he is unable to advance in any complete sense to Yesod, the link between body and mind. Once in possession of a theoretical understanding of the ten sefirah, the Kabbalist, through further study and meditation, and by learning how the tasks associated with the twenty-two paths between the individual sefirah can assist his progress, is able to begin in earnest his ascent through the tree. Such an ascent may form his life's work and few reach the end of it, but once in Kether one can know God and move beyond symbolism to experience infinity itself.

The House as Man
The dynamics of the sefiroth can be applied to any organism, system or transaction. In this 17th-century print, the design of a house and human anatomy are interpreted according to the principles of the tree of life.

Astrology

Mankind has always been fascinated by the stars. The ancients were intrigued by the motions and configurations of heavenly bodies, associating them with the mystic powers that governed human fate. In modern astronomy, the old deterministic views of the universe are falling into disfavour, and our awe of the cosmos remains undiminished.

In the earliest, tribal communities celestial phenomena were of great practical significance. Seasons were measured by the succession of longest and shortest days and the times of year when day and night were of equal length. This simple calendar became the basis of planting and hunting. As increasingly detailed celestial records were kept, stars were grouped together into constellations, and the movements of the heavenly bodies were monitored. In time, the constellations became associated with particular objects, animals and mythical figures, and human and divine qualities were projected onto the motions of sun, moon and planets. The skies came alive with imagery of gods, creatures and heroes, and a host of stories relating to this imagery was handed down through the generations. These tales gradually acquired deep mystical significance in explaining mankind's fate, and later still in analysing human character.

These connections between earth and universe become more credible when we remember that the ancients saw creation as a vast web of interconnected forces. Nothing was uninfluenced by what took place around it, no matter how great the distances concerned. The entrails of a sacrificial animal could indicate the outcome of a battle taking place in a far country; the future was foreseen in dreams; and a handful of stones cast on the ground could guide a person's actions. Human lives were a reflection of the realities written in the heavens.

Astrology – the divinatory system based on the interpretation of planetary configurations – had its earliest roots in Babylonian civilization. Tablets dating back to the 7th century BC set out the influence on human affairs of four celestial deities – Shamash (the sun), Sin (the moon), Ishtar (the planet Venus) and Adad (the weather god). Over the centuries, these Mesopotamian divinatory principles were transmitted through the Middle East, India and China, where they then developed independently, but it was not until the Hellenistic age that further significant advances were made in the science of astrology. In the 2nd century AD Ptolemy named the constellations as we know them today. Improved methods of observation then allowed Greek scholars to map the movement of the planets relative to fixed coordinates in the celestial sphere (the visible heavens), rather than to the local sphere (the four compass bearings). The constellations thus formed a backdrop against which the apparent motions of the sun, moon and planets (five of which could be seen in ancient times) were charted. The sun and planets appeared to move (relative to the stars) within a

Zodiacal Images
The images associated with the twelve signs of the zodiac were originally linked with the constellations. The signs are symbolized graphically by means of sigils, which accompany these images taken from a translation of a 15th-century Arabic text.

Zodiacal Man
The idealized body of celestial man was regarded as a microcosm of heavenly principles, and each sign of the zodiac was associated with a particular bodily function. Events above, such as the position of a planet in a sign, were mirrored below in a person's physical and mental well-being. Zodiacal man was a common theme throughout medieval literature (this image is from a 15th-century French manuscript): by the 16th century the relationship between astrology and the human body was well developed, and a patient's "humour" and ailments were diagnosed according to his or her birth sign.

narrow band of the sky, and this belt (or zodiac) was divided into twelve arcs of 30°, each corresponding to one of the twelve zodiacal signs. The signs were originally named after the most prominent constellations that fell within them. However, as a result of the natural "wobble" of the earth on its axis over the millennia, the constellations have shifted out of their signs. So, for example, at the beginning of the year, the sun no longer appears in Capricornus but in Saggitarius.

In the development of astrology, celestial movements were matched with terrestrial cycles, and the zodiac acquired a system of symbols that denoted conditions on earth according to the part of the sky in which the sun appeared. For example, at the height of summer, Leo (the lion) signified the sun's fiery heat. This sign is followed by Virgo (the virgin), symbolic of the harvesting of seed for next year's planting. Libra (the scales) represented the equilibrium between summer and winter, the time of the autumnal equinox, when day and night are of equal length.

Even in Ptolemy's time, the Greeks noted that people appeared to fall into categories of personality governed by the season of their birth. Gradually there evolved descriptions of twelve personality types corresponding approximately to the signs of the zodiac, and from these came the idea of individual horoscopes based on time of birth and various other more complex factors. Fatalistic astrology has persisted to this day in more or less the same form.

Planetary Influence
Mercury, depicted here in a 16th-century edition of *The Shepheard's Kalendar*, was seen as a male planet, influencing communication. Those born under Mercury were believed to be alert, quick-witted, fluent, with a tendency towards science.

The twelve signs of the zodiac are arranged into four groups of three, and each group is associated with a particular element (fire, water, air or earth) and with a particular quality and gender. The fire signs (Aries, Leo and Sagittarius) are linked to thrusting, energetic characteristics; the water signs (Pisces, Cancer and Scorpio) to emotional and intuitive traits; the air signs (Aquarius, Gemini and Libra) to characteristics of logic and intellect; and the earth signs (Capricorn, Taurus and Virgo) to practicality and dependability. Fire and air signs are, in addition, seen as extroverted, and water and earth signs as introverted.

The qualities of the signs, or quadruplicities, are either cardinal, fixed or mutable, reflecting the three basic qualities of life – creation (cardinal), preservation (fixed) and destruction (mutable). Cardinal signs are active and initiate events; fixed signs are passive and hold events on course; mutable signs make way for change. The signs are also divided according to gender, alternating between "masculine" and "feminine". Finally, the twelve signs can be divided into six pairs or "polarities" (Aries–Libra, Taurus–Scorpio, Gemini–Sagittarius, Cancer–Capricorn, Leo–Aquarius, and Virgo–Pisces), with each pair existing in balance.

The influence on earth of the heavenly bodies was thought to depend on the positions of the planets within the signs; and because the planets were seen as the driving forces behind people and events on earth, they were closely linked with the gods. Each planet (ten

Sun and Moon

Both sun and moon are
regarded as planets for the
purposes of astrology. The
moon represents the
imaginative and reflective
mind, while the sun symbolizes
the true essence of being. The
dark part of the lunar disk,
invisible when we see the
bright crescent, is a symbol of
the unconscious. The moon is
often associated with the sea,
and this 15th-century Italian
miniature shows it guiding
sailors on their voyage.

The Planetary Symbols

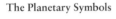

⊙ Sun

☽ Moon

☿ Mercury

♀ Venus

♂ Mars

♃ Jupiter

♄ Saturn

♅ Uranus

♆ Neptune

♇ Pluto

in all, as the sun and moon are counted as planets for astrological purposes) has a symbol and is said to "rule" one or more of the signs. The positions of the planets relative to one another, as seen from the earth, determine the interaction of the forces which the planets represent: these forces can work together when the planets are in approximately the same place in the sky (in conjunction), or against each other when the planets are separated by 90°.

For the purpose of casting a horoscope, the sky – that is, the local rather than celestial sphere – is divided into twelve units or "houses" relative to the horizon. The houses are numbered rather than named, and give clues to aspects of an individual's life, such as personal relationships, health, work and creativity, dependent upon which signs and planets are located within them.

The characteristics of each sign, the planetary influences and the areas defined by the houses, work together to produce a complex web of interrelation-ships, some complementary, some in opposition, all of which are said to determine the fate of mankind. Science has denied these connections for centuries and has held that the constellations which the ancients identified consist of heavenly bodies distanced from each other by vast tracts of space, and so remote from our own world that the possibility of their having any connection with our lives is out of the question. Astrology is thus seen as a pseudo-science, at best a crude fore-runner of modern astronomy. Yet the belief that our destiny is in some ways bound up with the stars persists. Clearly the symbolic system which astrology represents has a powerful hold upon our consciousness.

Certain recent trends in scientific thought are less dismissive. For example, modern physics no longer takes the view that the universe consists of a collection of separate bundles of matter. Creation is seen increasingly as a web of interconnected energy forms, an idea akin in some ways to the world-view of the ancients.

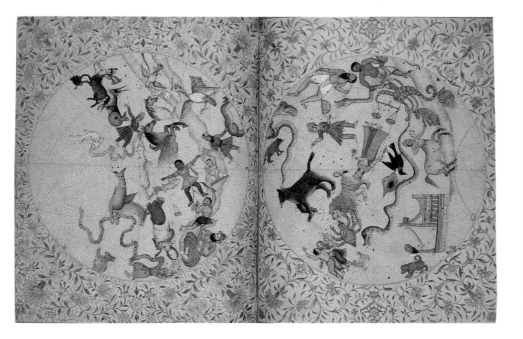

Star Maps
Star charts date from the earliest of civilizations. Primitive calendars were based on celestial records organized according to groups of stars, or constellations, that were easy to recognize. These stellar groups were overlaid with representations of animals or mythological characters familiar to that particular society. Ptolemy later catalogued more than 1,000 stars into 48 constellations, and Greek astronomy was transmitted to India via Sanskrit manuscripts, which included star maps such as this one. Ptolemy's system forms the basis of modern cartographic representations of the stars.

And although the gravitational pull and the light from all heavenly bodies other than the sun and moon are too feeble to exert any influence upon us, it is by no means certain that this is true of other electromagnetic sources out in space. Powerful magnetic fields exist throughout the solar system, and the earth's atmosphere is constantly bombarded by the solar wind, a stream of sub-atomic particles from the sun. The solar wind and the magnetic fields of the various planets in our solar system seem to influence each other in a variety of subtle and as yet imperfectly understood ways. Farther afield, the background radiation in what was once thought to be empty space is now believed to be a remnant from the "Big Bang" of universal creation. Thus, the argument that there are no scientific *mechanisms* to account for any influence the heavens may have upon the direction of human lives is becoming less plausible, particularly when the ability of fish, birds and other life-forms to navigate by the earth's magnetic field indicates that the nervous systems of living organisms may be highly sensitive to electromagnetic influences.

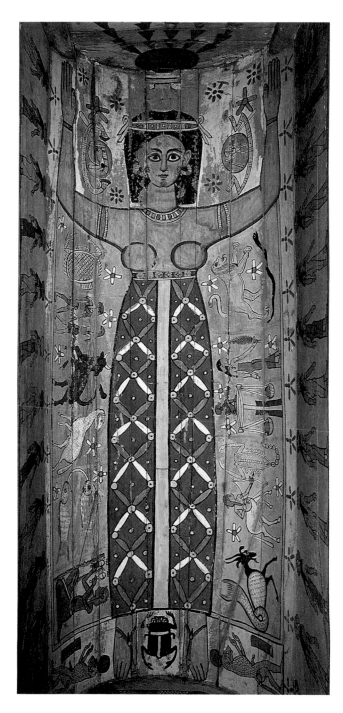

The Sky Goddess
In Egyptian mythology, Nut was goddess of the sky. She was often depicted as a woman with an elongated body, touching the earth with her fingertips and toes and bending over the globe, thus forming the arch of the heavens. The Milky Way was believed to be her star-covered belly. Nut became protectress of the dead, and her image was often to be found on the inner lid of sarcophagi. This wooden coffin from the early 2nd century AD shows Nut surrounded by signs of the zodiac, watching protectively over the mummified body.

The Fire Signs

Aries
Dates: March 21st – April 19th
Symbol: The Ram
Ruler: Mars

Aries is fire in its primitive form – impulsive, energetic, dynamic, initiatory, exploratory, but potentially uncontrolled and destructive. The energy of Aries needs some outside force to help channel it, and this is provided by Mars, the sign's ruler, which symbolizes a person's consciousness of himself, his individual nature which distinguishes him from the rest of humanity. The sigil (below) is a representation of the ram's horns, or of the human nose and eyebrows, the latter symbolizing our individual nature.

The ram's qualities are well known: brave and fierce, it puts down its head and charges with great determination at things that arouse its attention. The rushing ram also represents the first burst of growth in the crops at the onset of spring. Aries is the renewal of solar energy, and is traditionally seen as the first sign of the zodiac. The Arab astronomer Abumasar believed that Creation occurred when the sun, moon, Mercury, Venus, Mars, Jupiter and Saturn were all in conjunction (in the same part of the sky) in Aries.

Leo
Dates: July 23rd – August 21st
Symbol: The Lion
Ruler: Sun

Leo is fire in its controlled, fixed aspect, burning with a steady glow that illuminates and warms all who come into contact with it. The lion symbolizes life, strength, vigour, regal dignity, pride and courage. It is the king of the beasts, ruled by the most powerful of the planets, the sun. Leo denotes a clearer, steadier kind of authority than that of Aries, and is also linked with ambition, which in extreme forms can manifest itself as tyranny. The lion is one of the most ubiquitous symbols of power, masculinity and leadership, as evidenced by its presence in countless coats of arms.

Leo, a fixed sign, maintains the heat at the height of summer, which ripens the crops ready for harvest. The sign thus represents the life-giving, all-seeing Father at the centre of things, whence all energy flows and all life issues. The two circles in Leo's sigil (below) represent the link between the divine will and that of mankind.

The Water Signs

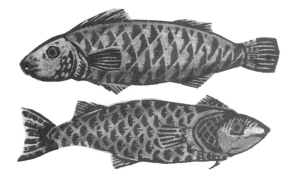

Sagittarius
Dates: November 22nd – December 21st
Symbol: The Centaur/Archer
Ruler: Jupiter

The third of the fire types possesses the qualities of the other two, but in a more purified and expansive form. Thus, Sagittarius has the initiatory power of Aries, but the ways in which that power is put into effect are more directed and refined. The ambition and dominance of Leo are turned toward more spiritual, less egotistical ends. The immortal Centaur represents the combination of the higher mental powers of mankind and the physical strength of the horse. The sigil (below) represents the moral foundation on which civilization may be built, the arrow of inspiration.

The archer symbolizes a purposeful nature, the ability to hit the target – the bow and arrow are symbols of power. Like Aries and Leo, Sagittarius is a leadership sign, but is also associated with sensitivity, an openness to the needs and ideas of others. Sagittarius embodies a restlessness that comes partly from the exploratory spirit shared with Aries, but also from the questing, spiritual side of the Sagittarian character. It is the last sign before the New Year and marks the transition between autumn and winter.

Pisces
Dates: February 20th – March 20th
Symbol: The Fishes
Ruler: Neptune/Jupiter

Water is deep, mysterious, capable of stillness and calm: in modern psychology it symbolizes the energy of the unconscious. Just as Aries is fire in its primitive form, so Pisces is water in its most fluid form. The Piscean character is emotional, sensitive, vague and unworldly, given to the mysterious world of dreaming and attracted to the unknown. At the same time, like water, the Piscean character is highly adaptable, able to accommodate itself to demanding situations. Water also suggests the flow toward other people, and this too is an aspect of Pisces – a gentle, compassionate nature, which can show itself as vulnerability.

Pisces is a time of year when the rains of late winter and early spring prepare the earth for a burst of activity in spring (Aries).

At its simplest level, the sigil (below) represents the fishes. In a more esoteric interpretation, one arc represents the finite consciousness of mankind, the other the consciousness of the universe. The line bisecting the arcs is the earth, the point at which the spiritual and material spheres of life meet.

Cancer
Dates: 23rd June – 23rd July
Symbol: The Crab
Ruler: The Moon

Cancer is water in its stiller, more controlled aspect. The Cancerian character, like the Piscean, is sensitive, affectionate and emotional, but less vulnerable in relations with others, and more prepared to communicate socially. Ruled by the moon, Cancer has a temperamental aspect, as well as possessing the depths associated with all water signs.

Other qualities denoted by Cancer are independence of spirit, soundness, calmness, clarity of vision and dependability. Stillness suggests a love of tradition, but the sign (like all water signs) has a strong, imaginative, intuitive side.

Cancer is the World Mother: in Greek mythology, the crab was given its place in heaven by Hera, the mother goddess. It is the time of the summer solstice, one of the most significant events in the yearly cycle. Ancient philosophers equated Cancer with the "gate of men" through which the soul descended from heaven and entered the human body. The sigil (below) represents the union of male and female principles (sperm and egg).

Scorpio
Dates: October 23rd – November 21st
Symbol: Scorpion/Eagle
Ruler: Mars/Pluto

The deepest and most emotional sign of the zodiac, Scorpio embodies the calmness of all water signs, as well as intense powers of self-discipline. Orientated toward the inner world, the Scorpio character has the intuitive abilities of Pisces alongside the steadfastness and clarity of Cancer. The sign symbolizes an intense and often withdrawn personality, tenacious in following its objectives.

The scorpion represents an ability to sting others, either through perception of their weaknesses, or through the ability to inspire them. Combining the powers of water and air, the eagle stands for an ability to achieve spiritual transformation, and to reach the heights and depths of inner understanding.

Mars brings to Scorpio great strength of purpose, while Pluto can bring jealousy and possessiveness. During the time of Scorpio, a fixed sign, autumn is well established. Animals retreat (from the scorpion) into hibernation through which they are regenerated. The sigil (below) represents the male reproductive organs, and completes the part-serpent symbolized by Virgo (see page 167).

♋

♏

The Air Signs

Aquarius

Dates: January 21st – February 19th
Symbol: The Water Carrier
Ruler: Saturn/Uranus

Aquarius shows the element air in its freest, most pervasive form. This gives the Aquarian character a sense of universality, which leads to good works and helping others. In fact, Aquarius is the most humanitarian sign in the zodiac – compassionate, visionary, hopeful, imbued with a sense of community and shared purpose. Yet in spite of this social dimension, there is also a reticence, partly due to the presence of Saturn in the sign.

The water carried by Aquarius is the water of knowledge, and symbolizes a desire not only to acquire learning but also to share it. The two jagged lines of the sigil (below) can symbolize the serpents of wisdom – intuition and rationality – or may be interpreted as waves on the water of consciousness, representing communication. Aquarian love of learning is said to be helped by the presence of Uranus as joint-ruler of the sign. Uranus also contributes an original and inventive turn of mind, a propensity toward science and technology, and a clear-cut approach to problem-solving.

Gemini

Dates: 22nd May – 23rd June
Symbol: The Heavenly Twins
Ruler: Mercury

Whereas Aquarius is air in its searching, pervasive aspect, Gemini is air in its changeable, whimsical, mercurial form. Sometimes referred to as the most child-like sign of the zodiac, Gemini exhibits a great need to relate to others. The sign symbolizes contradictions, the twins denoting a tendency to go to opposite extremes. The Gemini character, being adaptable, is content with its own paradoxical nature. Like all air signs, Gemini has stronger links with the intellect than with the emotions.

The sigil (below), which resembles the Roman numeral II, traditionally symbolizes duality. The Spartans used it to depict their twin gods as they went into battle. It suggests the joining of two souls, one intuitive, one rational, in order to achieve greater creativity, or the unity of mind and spirit.

The Earth Signs

Libra

Dates: September 23rd – October 22nd
Symbol: Scales
Ruler: Venus

As the symbol suggests, Libra is the sign most closely associated with justice. The Libran character combines the humanitarianism of Aquarius with the curiosity of Gemini, holding these and other qualities in a state of balance. Like other air signs, Libra embodies the intellect, but its innate balance prevents the strictly rational approach to life from overwhelming the intuitive. It also represents equilibrium between physicality and spirituality.

The presence of Venus as ruling planet links Libra with beauty, order, and a feeling for harmony that is the basis for peace-making. The negative side of Libran balance is a tendency to indecision.

The sigil (below) represents the sun sinking on the horizon, as night comes to dominate in the yearly cycle. The upper line symbolizes higher mental powers, while the lower line stands for material existence.

Capricorn

Dates: 23rd December – 19th January
Symbol: The Goat
Ruler: Saturn

Capricorn is the essence of earth, associated with stability and structure. This renders the Capricorn character cautious, practical and orderly. But the goat also symbolizes stubbornness or, in its more positive aspects, determination and self-discipline.

The presence of Saturn provides a calming influence, infusing the Capricorn personality with a deliberate, serious manner – the basis of good scholarship. The ruling planet, Saturn, brings a liking for solitude, and occasionally a dark, depressive side. The mystical side of Capricorn is most likely to express itself as an interest in earth mysteries and the hidden forces of nature. The original symbol for Capricorn – the goat-fish rather than mountain goat – was a mythical creature, which had access to great wisdom from having all the earth's resources – land and sea – at its disposal. The sigil (below) represents the dual nature of land and sea.

During the time of Capricorn, the earth proceeds into winter, and life looks inward in preparation for the spring. This is the time of the winter solstice, and Carpricorn is the "gate of the gods", as the sun starts to ascend once more.

Taurus
Dates: April 20th – May 19th
Symbol: The Bull
Ruler: Venus

Taurus is earth in its more visible, above-ground aspect. The stubbornness of Capricorn is here expressed not as defensiveness but as courage and strength. Like the bull, Taurus is fiery, difficult and determined, but at other times the dependable, capable side of the bull comes to the fore.

The influence of Venus as ruler means that the Taurean has a keen eye for natural beauty. Venus is also said to contribute a strong sexual motivation; and this, together with the earth aspect and the fertile power of the bull, gives rise to a strong sensuality, held in check only by the natural caution associated with the sign. There is a jealous and possessive side to Taurus, but also a seam of generosity and kindness.

The sigil (below) has the form of a full moon and a crescent. The full moon represents the celestial mother with attendant principles of growth and fertility, while the upturned crescent denotes the gathering of material possessions. Taurus depicts mankind bound to the earth. With spring at its peak, it represents also the full realization of the creative forces of nature.

Virgo
Dates: August 22nd – September 22nd
Symbol: The Virgin
Ruler: Mercury

Virgo is the sign of application. While Capricorn is associated with the inner places of the earth and Taurus with the surface, Virgo is more concerned with how the earth is made and the uses to which it may be put. It stands for transformation, a taking apart of the earth to study its nature, and then a moulding and changing of its shape to suit human needs.

The Virgoan character is analytical, and can often be overly critical. The symbol of the virgin stands for a tendency to discriminate too closely, and thus to reject all suitors on the grounds of their inadequacy, real or imagined. This can make the Virgoan personality uncomfortable for others, especially as the presence of Mercury as ruling planet contributes a restless, nervy tension. On the positive side, Virgo is associated with dependability and sincerity, combining the strength of the deep places of the earth with the fertility and abundance of the surface. It signifies great activity on the land, as man harvests the rewards of his labours

The sigil (below) represents the female reproductive parts, or the head and part-body of a serpent.

The Tarot

The Tarot cards are in effect two packs in one: the *major arcana*, which consist of twenty-two trump cards, each one unique; and the *minor arcana*, which differ from modern playing cards only in that the court cards in each of the suits are four in number (king, queen, knight and page or princess) instead of three, and that the suits themselves are pentacles (or coins), cups, wands and swords. It seems likely that the two packs were once separate, and were brought together because they served a common purpose – of which more in a moment.

The origins of the Tarot remain a mystery. Attempts have been made to trace it back variously to the ancient civilizations of Egypt, India and China, and its introduction into Europe has been credited to both the Arabs and the Gypsies (Romanies). Another theory is that the minor arcana were based, in part at least, upon unknown sets of cards brought back by Venetian traders from the East some time prior to the 15th century, and associated with the Hindu god Vishnu. Vishnu is traditionally shown with four arms and holding the disc, lotus, club and conch which symbolize the divine powers of preservation (*karma yoga*), love (*bhakti yoga*), wisdom (*gnana yoga*) and inner realization (*raja yoga*). These four symbols may be the origin of the four suits of the minor arcana.

If this is the case, the cards of the minor arcana were intended not as playing cards but as allegories of the soul's journey along four parallel paths toward spiritual enlightenment. In the course of this journey the individ-

Game Cards

Les Tarots was the name given to a French card game that was the forerunner of bridge. Its Italian equivalent was Tarocchi. This Tarocchi set is a late 19th-century design, and includes the major arcana, cards 12–21.

ual progresses through the stages represented by each numbered card and court card to the ultimate level of kingship. The major arcana, which probably also came to Venice from the East, may have been designed to show a more esoteric and profound spiritual route in which the four paths of the minor arcana are integrated into one. How the two packs became combined into one is unclear. Recognizing their similar purpose, occultists in northern Italy may have used them as alternatives, with the result that over the years they became more and more closely identified with each other, until the distinction between them disappeared. Certainly during this period the cards went through many modifications until they attained something like their present form.

The first recorded pack to resemble modern packs was made for the Duke of Milan in 1415, though some claim that the seventeen Tarot cards held in the Bibliothèque Nationale in Paris are remnants of a deck known to have been made for Charles VI of France in 1392. Whichever of these is the more ancient, it is certain that from the early 15th century the cards came to be widely used in France as well as in Italy, and eventually spread throughout Europe. In the course of time their original intention became overlaid by their role as playing cards, and because the major arcana proved too complex for this purpose, they disappeared from what is now the modern playing pack.

There is a strong tradition that locates the Tarot's origins in the body of universal knowledge laid down

THE WORLD.

JUDGEMENT.

The Waite Pack

The Waite pack in many ways revolutionized the Tarot in the 20th century. Designed by Arthur Edward Waite, a member of the Hermetic Order of the Golden Dawn (see page 144), and painted by Pamela Colman, the Waite (or "Rider") pack set an example followed by many later packs. The cards of the minor arcana show scenes rather than merely the number of symbols from the suit, and this extends the scope of the diviner in his or her interpretation of the images. This is one reason for the pack's popularity around the world, despite a proliferation of other Tarot packs during the last twenty-five years.

by the Egyptian god Thoth for his disciples in magic. Inspired by this theory, a Paris wigmaker who called himself Etteila (his real name spelled in reverse) devised his own Tarot pack for divination purposes. This was taken up in the mid-19th century by Eliphas Lévi (the occult pseudonym of Alphonse Louis Constant) who extended Etteila's ideas into a complete system, based on Egyptian images, but linked also with the Kabbalah.

Although Lévi's interpretation is based on suspect premises, the Kabbalistic echoes of the Tarot are undeniable. For example, the twenty-two letters of the Hebrew alphabet correspond with the twenty-two major arcana of the Tarot; and the four suits of the minor arcana could be said to reflect the four Kabbalistic "worlds", the four steps by which God created the cosmos. Lévi's theories were a significant influence on Arthur Edward Waite (see above), who devised one of the most popular packs in use today.

The major arcana constitute one of the most intriguing of all symbol systems, combining mysteries of the past with a complex and powerful system of inner growth. To spend time with the Tarot and identify with its images is to commence a journey of self-discovery that can leave the individual profoundly changed. The twenty-two cards of the major arcana are a symbolic synopsis of our own nature. One way of expressing this is that they are an attempt to represent the factors that go to make up our personality, an attempt which pre-dates the efforts of modern psychologists by more than five hundred years.

Working with the Tarot

In order to make use of the major arcana as a method of self-discovery, it is necessary to spend time reflecting on what each of the twenty-two cards represents. Read the descriptions given in the following pages, then take one card at a time, and for several days allow your mind to return to it as often as you can. Put the card somewhere prominent and look at it as often as possible. Allow the image to become firmly fixed in your mind, so that you are able to visualize it in detail and hold it in your mind as you drift into sleep each night. Ask the central figure (or figures) in the image what it has to tell you about yourself. Don't worry whether you are talking to an image that has objective reality or simply to an aspect of your own unconscious. In all work with symbols, results come only if we cease to plague ourselves with the need for logical explanations. The image is simply there, existing in its own dimension. Let the image do the work for you.

In this way, use each of the twenty-two cards in turn. Take them in the order in which they appear in the pack, from The Fool to The World. Don't allow personal preferences for certain cards to influence you unduly. Note these preferences, and then put them to one side. Don't regard some cards as "good" and others as "bad". Each has its part to play.

You may need to stay longer with some cards than with others, but after a time each card will start to stimulate self-insights. Some of these will be very clear, as if that aspect of yourself is already well known and accepted by you. Others will be more shadowy. Note the fact: this is an important discovery in itself. When you feel that a card has revealed all it can for now, move on, but don't rush things. Stay with each card until a conviction arises that you have grasped its message. Draw or paint the card to help it speak directly to your unconscious. Once you can visualize it clearly with eyes closed, sit in a relaxed but upright position and meditate deeply upon it by holding it in your awareness and disregarding any extraneous thoughts. When you can concentrate upon it to the exclusion of all else, imagine that the frame around the image is the frame of a door, and that you are looking out onto the scene in front of you. Then step through the door and become part of the scene. Notice how at this point events may take on a life of their own, as they do in a dream. Allow the scene to unfold around you, and see what happens.

When you have worked through all twenty-two cards, you will have a deeper and richer awareness of aspects of yourself. Analyse this awareness. Are there aspects of yourself that are clearly undeveloped and need more freedom? Are there other aspects which arouse shame? Are there aspects that are obvious strengths, and can be allowed more space to flourish?

You may have noticed, as you proceeded through the cards, a cumulative effect of insights from the earlier cards being carried into your work with the later ones. All the cards have their role to play, but the order in which you face them is important. You cannot proceed properly to card number one, The Magician, until you have recognized in yourself the innocence, the "don't know mind" (as Zen Buddhism puts it) of the first, unnumbered card, The Fool. And you cannot proceed properly to card number two, the High Priestess, until you have recognized The Magician within yourself, your own inner power to transform and change.

Divination

For many people, the best-known use of the major arcana (some systems employ the minor as well) is as a means of divination. The cards are shuffled, spread face down in a certain way, and then turned up one by one in order to reveal certain things about the personality of someone present, or to provide advice about problems or insights into the future. Nevertheless, it is well to remember, when using the Tarot for divination, that occult tradition claims other, superior purposes for it. In divination each card is interpreted by the diviner, instead of revealing itself more fully through meditation and study. At the end of each of the descriptions that follow, are some of the divinatory meanings usually attached to each card, but if you wish to use the pack for this purpose you should first go through the process described above, so that each card is allowed to come properly alive for you. It hardly needs saying that divination is best done for oneself, rather than by another person.

When using the cards for divination, you need to reverse some by turning those you hold in your hand through ninety degrees each time you cut the pack. When you lay the cards in a spread and begin the process of divination, any card which is reversed when turned face-up represents negative aspects of the qualities concerned. Within the spread, each card is also influenced by those adjacent to it. Thus a positive card may be hindered by negative (reversed) cards, while the effects of a negative card may be lessened by positive ones. However, two positive cards may cancel each other out if they are clearly carrying conflicting messages, and the same can be true of two negative cards. Remember always that when answering questions about the future the cards are giving advice, not saying what is bound to happen. Nothing seen in the cards is inevitable, and negative cards should be taken as a warning rather than as certain indicators of ill-fate.

0. The Fool

In the medieval world the fool was not always viewed as a simpleton. As the court jester, he was seen as possessing a naive wisdom that made him wiser at times than those around him. In addition, he was allowed to break the rules of court etiquette. He was outside the system, laughed at but in a strange way privileged. The fool, like Socrates, was wise enough to know that he knew nothing. His mind was not overloaded with preconceptions and definitions. He saw things as they were. In the Tarot, The Fool is that part of ourselves that is wise enough to stand awestruck before the mystery of creation, and bold enough to set off exploring. The Fool is the only card in the major arcana that is unnumbered, and he has no set position in the order of the cards. He symbolizes the part of us that looks out upon the thoughts, feelings and dreams playing across the shadow theatre of the mind. Carrying the minimum of possessions and the pilgrim's staff, egged on by a strange animal (sometimes a cat or dog) symbolizing the inner motivation that snaps at our heels once we start to question the nature of reality, The Fool steps toward the unknown – the inner self.

Divinatory meaning: unplanned incident or endeavour; unexpected new beginning of some kind. Can turn out well if flanked by fortunate cards, otherwise can indicate an unwise move. *Reversed*: impetuous foolishness.

LE·BATELEUR

LA PAPESSA

L'IMPERATRIS

I. The Magician

Magic is essentially the process of transformation. Without some inner magic, our real self is doomed to lie forever hidden under the confused world of emotions, physical needs and social conditioning. The Magician (also called The Juggler) is the part of ourselves that inaugurates this transformation.

On the table in front of The Magician is a collection of implements: some packs show the pentacle, the chalice, the wand and the sword, symbolizing respectively existence, love, wisdom and inner realization, and also the four elements that make up not only the world but our own bodies. The pentacle and the cup also represent the female, inner, receptive side of existence, while the wand and the sword symbolize the male, outer, penetrative side. Without the union of female and male there is no creation.

Divinatory meaning: planned or foreseen new beginning. Self-confidence, strength of will, readiness to take risks. *Reversed*: weakness of will, inability to take new opportunities.

II. The High Priestess

Every symbol system of any value reminds us that male and female are equal, complementary aspects of a universal whole. Only through an understanding of this can we progress to a proper balance within both society and the individual self.

The High Priestess embodies the hidden, mystic, receptive feminine principle that awaits the energy of the overt, active, male principle. For the ancients the priest-king, the ruler of the visible world, was balanced by the high priestess, the ruler of the invisible world. We can only undertake the developmental journey of the major arcana by acknowledging what the high priestess symbolizes within ourselves. She sits, enigmatic and beautiful, and holds the book of wisdom on her knee. She is the oracle and knows the answers to all questions.

Divinatory meaning: intuitive insight, creative abilities, revelation of hidden things. *Reversed*: emotional instability, enslavement to a woman, lack of insight.

III. The Empress

The High Priestess shows one aspect of female power. Another is shown by The Empress, the bringer of maternal fertility, the earth-mother presiding over the creation and destiny of sons and daughters. On her head is a diadem representing the gifts we receive at birth, and on her shield is an eagle, a symbol of heaven and the sun, and a host of positive attributes including courage and clear vision.

The Empress is not mysterious but open, and addresses those who seek the truth. She represents the conscious mind and unites matter and spirit. Her sceptre shows that she rules heaven, earth and the world in between, but it is merely a symbol: only through actual union with the male can the secret of The Empress's power be revealed in its completeness, at both the mystical and the earth-mother level.

Divinatory meaning: fertility, abundance, growth, strength from nature and the natural world, comfort and security. *Reversed*: impoverishment, stagnation, domestic upheaval.

IIII. The Emperor

The next pair of cards represents the masculine sides of our nature. The Emperor is the archetype of male power – of strength, leadership and achievement. In his hands he holds the phallic symbols of male energy, the orb and the sceptre, which also denote his power to guide the world. Within the material world over which The Emperor rules there is the hidden spiritual world, which is attainable only when the male is united with the female, symbolized by the circle crowning the sceptre's shaft. The Empress and Emperor combine complementary aspects of a divine unity.

Unlike The Empress, The Emperor in some packs wears armour, the armour of the male which protects him in worldly battles but at the same time prevents him from revealing his vulnerability, his feelings, his weaker self. Without such a revelation the male principle remains always defensive, unable to self-disclose.

Divinatory meaning: vigour, self-control, ambition, leadership, strength. *Reversed*: failure of ambition, weakness, subservience, loss of influence.

V. The Hierophant

The Hierophant, or priest, sometimes called the Pope, is male energy expressed as spiritual power, the feminine in the male. He is enthroned, like The Emperor, but his power over his fellows, as represented by the priests at his feet, comes from obedience not force. The masculine side still represents the external, exoteric type of spirituality, in contrast to the feminine side representing the internal and esoteric type. The Hierophant wears the red robe of external power: however, a blue robe (symbolizing internal power) shows under the red one.

On his head The Hierophant wears a triple-tiered crown, for he rules on three planes – physical, intellectual and divine. The symbolism of three is repeated in the triple cross in his left hand, indicating the mysteries of the godhead as revealed through the Trinity.

Divinatory meaning: knowledge, wisdom, inspirational help, wise counsel. *Reversed*: misinformation, slander, bad advice.

VI. The Lovers

In many Tarot packs this card shows a man flanked by two women, one pure and respectable, the other beautiful and wanton. The figure above their heads is Cupid, his arrow pointing variously at one of the three people below him. The symbolism is clear: having recognized the need for male to unite with female at the level of the inner self, the choice is now between the two versions of femininity: on the one hand the virginal and sacred (The Priestess), and on the other the fertile and material (The Empress).

The Waite pack shows a naked man and woman, with an androgynous winged figure above their heads – representing the coming together of the fully integrated male with the fully integrated female. The winged figure is that part of the inner self which is beyond male and female, and which both brings about, and is born from, the union of polar opposites.

Divinatory meaning: attraction, love, partnership, impending choice. *Reversed*: indecision, problems in a relationship, aversion.

VII. The Chariot

In the figure of the charioteer (often shown as female in early packs) there is something of the androgyne. The breastplate is the armour of maleness, but on the shoulders are the feminine lunar symbols. The charioteer is bound for the stars, the macrocosm, as emphasized in some packs by stars above and around his head and wings adorning the front of the chariot. The Waite pack shows a walled and turreted city in the background, but the charioteer faces away from it, turning his back on the material world and temporal power.

The Chariot is drawn by two horses in some packs, and by two sphinxes in others. One is male and one female, symbols respectively of all-knowledge and all-wisdom.

Divinatory meaning: deserved success, good progress, well-earned reward. *Reversed*: egocentricity, insensitivity, ruthlessness, progress at the expense of others.

VIII. Justice

MacGregor Mathers, creator of the Golden Dawn system of magic (see page 144), exchanged the position of this card (originally card XI) with that of Strength (see opposite).

There is a clear relationship between Justice, shown as a woman in all packs, and Strength. Strength shows the conquest of outer forces (symbolized by the lion), while Justice shows their assimilation by the conqueror. Justice wears the red robe of worldly power, and holds a sword and some scales. In the Tarot the sword symbolizes spiritual realization, not vengeance. Justice uses her power only to cut through those things that impede this realization. The scales allow her to weigh the value of all things and to maintain a balance between outer and inner, exoteric and esoteric.

Divinatory meaning: arbitration, negotiation, agreement, sound judgment. *Reversed*: injustice, prejudice, discord.

VIIII. The Hermit

At one level the Hermit represents the loneliness of the spiritual quest. The figure is elderly, because youth – or, rather, the pursuits of youth – have been sacrificed. But age is also a symbol of wisdom, of the realization that comes from experience, suffering and self-denial. At another level, The Hermit symbolizes perseverance, and the fact that each person must find enlightenment, the real self, the inner truth, by his or her unaided efforts.

In his right hand The Hermit holds a lantern, and the light inside can take the form of a star, a guide to help us through the darkness. In the left hand is the staff of the pilgrim, which is also the wand, the rod that drives out ignorance.

Divinatory meaning: discretion, silence, need for personal space or solitude, self-sufficiency in solving problems, self-reliance. *Reversed*: rejection of others or of advice, isolationism, obstinacy.

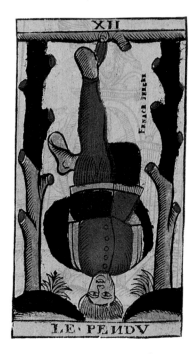

X. Wheel of Fortune

The wheel represents movement, and although we usually think of this movement as taking us forward, in fact each point on the wheel always returns to the same place. However, each time we return to a particular point we are potentially richer for having experienced the wheel's revolution. One day our experience will be such that we can step off the wheel, into the greater reality of which it is only a limited part.

In many Tarot packs, The Wheel of Fortune carries three mythical beings. At the left is a creature (often part monkey) ruled by instincts, and descending; at the right the animal (sometimes part hare) is intelligent, and climbs heavenward; at the top, the creature (often part sphinx) symbolizes spiritual knowledge. Waite, in his pack, adds in the corners of the card the four creatures of Ezekiel's vision mentioned in Revelations.

Divinatory meaning: good fortune, major events, big change in life circumstances. *Reversed*: end of a cycle of good fortune, turn for the worst.

XI. Strength

In some packs Strength is shown as male rather than female, but the struggle with the open-mouthed lion is almost invariable. The message of the card is that although strength may be symbolized by the raw energy of the lion, there is a higher strength which manifests itself through means other than the physical. The higher strength is spiritual strength, the awareness of the immortal, indestructible power inside us which transcends materiality and is not affected by its disintegration. In the Waite pack the woman wears garlands of flowers, echoing the symbolism of The Magician, and reminding us of the blossoming of the creative mind; and the symbol of life hovers over her head, as over the Magician's. In other packs both figures wear a hat in the shape of a "lazy eight", a symbol of infinity and boundless understanding.

Divinatory meaning: well-won triumph over others or over self, reconciliation, grasped opportunity. *Reversed*: defeat, surrender to baser instincts or to others, missed opportunity.

XII. The Hanged Man

The Hanged Man is suspended upside down in the traditional punishment meted out to debtors, yet his face is untroubled. He hangs on a gibbet, yet in some packs the gibbet bears the leaves of life. The crosspiece and uprights of the gibbet represent three, the number of creation; yet The Hanged Man's legs are crossed in a number four, the number of completion.

The Hanged Man symbolizes alignment with the laws of the universe and rebellion against the laws of mankind. The seeker after enlightenment must go his or her own way on the journey between creation and completion, whatever the cost. But since death on the tree was the Christian sacrifice, The Hanged Man also symbolizes selfless love.

Divinatory meaning: flexibility, self-sacrifice in a good cause, responsiveness to inner intuition, discarding of undesirable aspects of behaviour or of the ego. *Reversed*: unsuccessful inner struggle, refusal to respond to intuition or to abandon undesirable qualities.

XIII. Death

Death is not a final annihilation to be feared, but a necessary part of the cycle of existence: without death there would be no life. Thus, Death is not the last card but, with The Hanged Man, marks the transition from the first half of the pack to the second. The sacrifice of the ego, symbolized by The Hanged Man, frees us to cross the dark river Styx that divides the material from the spiritual world.

The image of Death, a skeleton carrying a scythe which symbolizes the severance and liberation of the self from the body, also carries the number thirteen, forbidding in itself. But death is part of the initiation into the spiritual world. In all mystery religions and shamanic traditions, the initiate had to undergo a secret ceremony in which he or she "died" and journeyed across the dark river to whatever lay beyond. Death brings us face to face with this transforming experience.

Divinatory meaning: blessing in disguise, end of prevailing negative situation, profound inner changes. *Reversed*: inertia, lethargy, stagnation.

XIIII. Temperance

After the trauma of The Hanged Man and Death, we come to a symbol of peace and tranquillity. Temperance is shown filling with the waters of new life the empty vessel left by the death of the ego. Losing the ego means stripping ourselves of misconceptions, pride, and the attachments and aversions we habitually show toward the transient experiences of material life. But once the ego is lost, something must be allowed to take its place. We cannot become hollow men and women, vulnerable to being invaded by a new ego of spiritual pride. The true reality inside ourselves has not yet had time to fill our whole being. Temperance therefore provides us with the sustenance we need in order to go further.

Divinatory meaning: skilful combination of circumstances achieved or necessary, circumspection, moderation. *Reversed*: inept combination of circumstances, competing interests, excess.

XV. The Devil

There are pitfalls even after achieving the death of the ego and receiving the sustenance of temperance. Crossing the Styx takes us into the world beyond the ego, but it does not take us into "heaven". Once outside the "safety" of the solid but illusory material world we are faced by the underworld as well as the higher world.

The Devil symbolizes the underworld, but the message is not one of evil but of trial. The Devil is, as it were, the quality controller. He raises his hand to halt progress, challenging us to look still deeper into ourselves. Unless we have been purged of the self and had our pride tempered, we may be in danger of taking the path of personal power.

Divinatory meaning: challenge, re-direction or transmutation of physical energy into more mental or spiritual pursuits. *Reversed*: repression of inner self, lust for material power and gain.

XVI. The Tower

If we fail the test set by The Devil, we are cast down to destruction. The crown of our achievement is placed on an edifice that crumbles under a bolt of lightning (divine justice). The lightning is not frightening, however, but beneficial and purifying. Neither is The Tower (or House of God) negative: it symbolizes a casting out of those remaining aspects of the self which are capable of fragmenting our essential unity of being.

Many packs show drops falling from the sky, which symbolize the positive energy that can come from destruction. It is no accident that this card is number sixteen in the series. One and six together give seven, and The Tower links back to card VII, The Chariot, and thus can be a card of progress and positive action.

Divinatory meaning: unexpected challenge, abrupt change in inner life, emotional release, purging of repressed feelings. *Reversed*: avoidable calamity, knocking off balance by events, severe emotional repression.

XVII. The Star

Having negotiated The Devil and The Tower, we now reach calmer pastures. The Star in many packs shows the clear links between this stage of the journey and Temperance. This time, however, the female figure has no need for wings, for she does not come from a higher realm to meet the traveller. Instead, the traveller has reached her level.

Like Temperance, The Star carries two pitchers, but instead of pouring from one into the other she empties one into a pool of water (the unconscious mind) and the other onto the ground (the conscious mind). The clear sky carries a single gold star surrounded by seven smaller stars. The overriding symbolism is that of rebirth. Having been purged of remnants of the ego by The Devil and in The Tower, we now experience rebirth in the higher realms of being.

Divinatory meaning: sudden widening of horizons, new life and vigour, deep insight. *Reversed*: reluctance to take broader view, lack of trust and openness, self-doubt.

XVIII. The Moon

The moon is a feminine symbol *par excellence*, and it reveals the mystical inner side of each of us in its full power. The final reconciliation is now poised to take place between the opposite poles that go to make up our own being, the male and the female, the conscious and the unconscious, the outer and the inner. The dogs pictured on the card are baying at the moon through ignorance of her true nature; they symbolize a psychic barrier to this inner reconciliation. The crayfish, the lower female element, emerges from the depths of the unconscious and through ignorance seeks to emasculate the male. But the light falling from the moon shows us that all may ultimately be well. The towers are a barrier only to those who, so near the end of their journey, draw back from full understanding.

Divinatory meaning: need to rely on intuition and imagination rather than reason; time for self-reliance. *Reversed*: fear of over-stepping safe boundaries, failure of nerve, fear of the unknown.

XIX. The Sun

Just as the moon is the root symbol of the feminine, so the sun is the root symbol of the male. Here in card nineteen we see The Sun in full splendour, and in many early Tarot packs its radiance falls upon a man and a woman (or Gemini, the Twins) in each other's arms. Full union has taken place, and the two have become one. The sense of alienation, separation and fragmentation which lies at the heart of human unease has disappeared at last.

However, the quester's journey is never-ending. The sun rises each morning. The cycle of life is eternal. Beyond the level reached in The Sun there are other levels to be traversed, high above human comprehension. For the moment, though, this is a pause. We can savour the triumph of the spirit.

There is a wall behind the figures which does not appear in all packs, but which provides some shade from the sun. The figures are facing *away* from the sun, as we are not yet ready to look fully into the face of ultimate reality. We are still, even at this stage, separate from it, and its full majesty would overpower us.

Divinatory meaning: success, achievement, triumph over odds, safety after peril, a just reward. *Reversed*: misjudgment, illusory success, exposure of success obtained by dubious means.

XX. The Judgment

Having come so far, is all that awaits us a judgment, which could send us back to the beginning again? The Judgment shows an angelic figure sounding a trumpet, and a grave apparently opening to release the dead. Is this card a representation of the Last Trump, when the human race itself is to be called to account? Or is it a symbol of resurrection, with everyone saved? If so, how does it relate to the cards that have gone before? Does it suggest that the attainment of enlightenment by one individual saves the whole race, just as Christians believe that Christ died to atone for our sins?

It is this last explanation that carries most symbolic force, and fits best with the teachings of many of the great spiritual traditions and with the other cards of the Tarot. The angelic figure thus represents the next stage in the spiritual journey. Having reached enlightenment, our need now is to turn back and rouse our fellows. This is the task of the bodhisattva in Buddhism, who having reached Nirvana, refuses to enter until the whole of the human race can enter as well.

Divinatory meaning: return to health, justified pride in achievement, a new lease of life. *Reversed*: punishment for failure, regret for lost opportunities.

XXI. The World

Here we see the supreme symbol of wholeness. Surrounded by the laurel wreath of victory, a naked woman holds a taper or a magician's wand. Above and below, the macrocosm and the microcosm, even right and left, have now become one. The figure is no longer confined by land or water, but stands in the supreme freedom of pure being.

Around the laurel wreath, the four creatures of Ezekiel occupy the corners of the card. The Tarot journey has reached completion. Whether teaching others or moving on to levels beyond comprehension, the aspirant is now free, and will never again return to the prison of ignorance.

The naked figure is no longer completely naked. A veil drapes itself across the body, hiding the genitals, the symbol of creativity. The veil reminds us again that there are more mysteries to come. And the number 21, though the occult number of completion (being 3 times 7, two numbers of magical significance), is not the number of absolute unity, infinity, unlimited potential. That number is zero, the number of The Fool, the card we met at the outset, which has accompanied us throughout our journey. The Fool is zero, the one who abandons concepts about reality in favour of direct experience.

Tantra

Tantra is not a religion, but a system of occult practices that infuses certain aspects of Hindu, Buddhist and Jain belief. The practioner, or *tantrika*, explores each of the energies of his own being, transforming them in the process into the subtler energies of the spirit. Tantra harnesses the exuberant extremes of life, in contrast to the more traditional spiritual path of denial. It accepts that, properly invoked, each of the creative energies within men and women is potentially spiritual energy. Only when each of these energies is acknowledged and allowed to unite with the other elements of the mind can men and women ascend to the ultimate state of being.

Erotic Energy

In the Tantric tradition, erotic symbolism is incorporated into art, from temple sculptures to yogic diagrams. This image from a Tantric manuscript of instruction on sexual practices typifies the exaltation of sexual energy as a means of spiritual growth.

The symbols used in Tantra are among the richest contained in any symbol system. The great cosmic diagram of the cult is the Sri Yantra (see page 60), which provides a focus for meditation enabling the *tantrika* to gaze upon the continuing process of creation. The divine figures Mahakala (Great Time) and Kali, the female embodiment of Time, serve as creative functions of the Supreme Truth. Kali is a grotesque goddess, whose hideousness must be accepted and welcomed by the adept.

The most striking Tantric symbols are those associated with sexuality. These are frequently taken in the West as evidence of depravity and licentiousness, but in fact they represent the fact that sexual energy can be used by the adept for the purposes of spiritual growth. In Tantra, sexual arousal can be used to hold the adept for long periods in the highest bliss the body can experience. This bliss is not dissipated in orgasm, but retained in the body in a subtler form, which can help the adept climb further up the ladder of spirituality.

The yoni (vulva) is a recurrent image in Tantric iconography, reflecting the view that the world's existence is a continuous birth. In parallel with this is the notion of continuous and ecstatic fertilization by the male seed. The male organ is represented by the lingam, and the female by various vulvic images such as the lotus flower. Creation is expressed in erotic terms as the union of Shiva and Shakti, which culminates in a dance by Shakti from which she weaves the world's fabric while Shiva looks on.

Also central to Tantrism is the idea of the subtle body, the basis of yogic practice. The adept visualizes the universe encircling the mythical Mount Meru, and then proceeds to identify his own spine with the mountain's central axis, so that he himself becomes cosmic. He locates each particular aspect of the world as flowing in a stream from his own being, and focuses these streams upon the chakras (see page 182) or lotuses – a string of power centres arranged in series within the subtle body. Hindu Tantra emphasizes the lowest lotus, where dwells the subtle serpent Kundalini. When awakened by yogic exercise, the serpent activates the energy of the central spine (Sushumna). Then Kundalini enters the higher lotuses in turn, until time is transcended and the reality beyond time experienced.

Tantric Iconography
This 18th-century Tibetan wall-hanging encapsulates Tantric symbolic art, and summarizes the system in which symbolic diagrams based on geometric shapes (and often spiritual figures) are used in meditation. The image includes the mandalas of the Wrathful Buddhas, the Peaceful Buddhas and the Knowledge-Holders.

The Chakras

The Sanskrit word *chakra* means "wheel". Usually depicted as seven in number, the chakras are said by the Tantric and yogic traditions to symbolize concentrated centres of the *prana* – the energy which, together with food and air, is needed to sustain our lives. Medical science has found no evidence for their existence, but this is hardly surprising, as it has always been claimed that they are located not in the physical but in the etheric body. In addition to the physical body, a man or woman is said to possess an etheric and an astral body, the former interpenetrating and extending just beyond the physical and providing the vehicle for prana, and the latter clothing the soul and providing the seat of consciousness. At death both the etheric and the astral bodies leave the physical, the etheric to disintegrate after three days, and the astral to go on to the next stage in life's journey.

Those who are sufficiently gifted are said to be able to see the etheric body as a fine mist surrounding the physical, the chakras appearing in spiritually undeveloped men and women as small discs about two inches in diameter and revolving slowly; and in more awakened beings as blazing miniature suns, much increased in size and spinning rapidly. Just enough pranic energy flows from the life force into the chakras of undeveloped individuals to sustain existence; while the awakened receive enormously enhanced energy streams which endow them with additional faculties and possibilities. The revolutions of the chakras set up secondary energy flows, which then circulate into and through the physical body along the meridians identified by acupuncturists, whose physical reality has been demonstrated to some extent by Western science.

In addition to the energy flowing into the chakras from the higher life-force, there is also said to be an earth energy which enters only at the base chakra. This derives from that portion of higher energy which has gone directly into the earth and then, having touched the lowest point of creation, is beginning to stream upward again (since all energy is cyclic) to rejoin its source. However, on entering the human body it is usually blocked by the undeveloped nature of the base chakra, and there it slumbers, the so-called serpent or Kundalini energy. In advanced beings this energy can be aroused and made to flow upward through the chakras. As it does so, it merges with the incoming higher energies until finally it reaches the crown chakra, where it explodes into the thousand-petalled lotus of light, giving the individual direct access to higher worlds.

Symbols of the Chakras
Each chakra is traditionally depicted as a lotus or wheel. At its centre is a Sanskrit inscription of the fundamental meditative note, together with the animal that symbolizes the forces of the chakra (an antelope in the case of the *Anahata*, or heart chakra, above).

Because the Kundalini energy is symbolized as female and the higher energies as male, this union of the two has obvious parallels with the male and female forces present in the Tarot, and with the chemical wedding of the alchemists. But there are dire warnings to be sounded. Unlike the gradual path of the Tarot, Kundalini energy can be roused relatively rapidly if one follows the right meditational practices. However, if this happens before the chakras

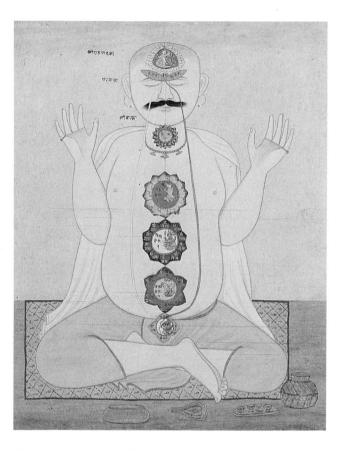

Chakras in the Subtle Body
This early 19th-century Indian diagram shows the system of
channels of energy flow and chakras in the etheric body. The
position of the chakras on the etheric body corresponds
approximately with that of certain physical organs: the base of the
spine, the genitals, the navel, the heart, the throat, the brow
(pituitary gland) and the crown (pineal gland). The first two are the
lower or physiological centres, sustaining primitive, animalistic
functions; the next three are the middle or personal centres, which
feed the emotions and those mental functions which together make
up the personality; and the final two are the higher or spiritual
centres, which in most people are said to be hardly developed at all.
Each chakra has a different colour associated with it, from red, the
colour of raw energy in the base chakra, through progressively
more spiritual colours, to white in the brow chakra. The crown is
sometimes represented as a blaze of brilliant colour.

themselves have been properly opened through moral
and spiritual development and through control of the
will and of the thoughts, the results are said to be real
and terrible, ranging from physical injury and even
death to grave damage to both etheric and astral
bodies. Far better to live and die with the Kundalini
unawakened than to arouse it prematurely.

Each chakra represents an element of ourselves,
from sexual desire at the lowest point through spiritual
fulfilment at the highest, and the chakras correspond
accurately to the hierarchy of developmental needs recognized by modern psychologists. The best-known representation of these needs is that proposed by the
American psychologist Abraham Maslow (1908–1970).
The first chakra symbolizes what Maslow terms basic
physiological needs, the second chakra safety needs, the
next three social, ego and autonomy needs respectively,
and the upper two the needs for self-actualization and
transcendence. The early yogis thus seem to be in start-
ling agreement with the ideas of modern psychologists.

But the yogis went further in devising a system of
meditation which helped the individual to open each of
the chakras in turn, moving progressively up through
the hierarchy to improve physical, psychological and
spiritual health. In one version of the system the yogi
meditates initially upon the base chakra, focusing attention upon the corresponding part of the physical body.
He visualizes the chakra expanding under an influx of
red light and sees it flowing through the whole physical
body, bringing renewed vitality and at the same time
becoming increasingly purified as it flows upward.
Once this visualization is fully established, attention is
switched upward to the next chakra and the process
repeated. The effectiveness of this meditation is
enhanced by leading a moral life, in which the practitioner consciously tries to strengthen the will by practising mindfulness and self-discipline.

I Ching

Do we live in a universe in which objects and events are individual and disconnected, or one where everything that happens is part of a single, vast, interrelated whole, an awesome stream of interconnections stretching from first causes into the remote future? Our present love of analysis and reductionism, suggest the former; mysticism, and the world-views of the ancients and of many modern theoretical physicists, suggest the latter. If the holistic view is correct, there is in a real sense no such thing as chance. Every happening, even the turn of a card or fall of a coin, is caused by a chain of preceding events, whether these be apparent to the senses or not.

The Sixty-four hexagrams
This 19th-century print shows the sixty-four symbolic hexagrams of the I Ching in a quadrate form.

of reality is based on these opposites, but acknowledges that the opposites are mutable and that nothing is permanent. In the trigrams, the two opposing combinations of three continuous lines (*Ch'ien*) and three broken lines (*K'un*) each progressively takes on aspects of the other (as shown, right) until the distinction between them disappears; and just as the trigrams flow into each other, so do their meanings.

At some point the eight trigrams were put together to form the sixty-four hexagrams, and these together were thought to represent all the basic human situations. To identify which of the sixty-four hexagrams provides the answer to a particular question, the questor takes three small coins (easier to come by than yarrow sticks) and tosses them six times in succession. The combination of heads and tails produced each time determines whether to select a continuous or a broken line: thus, three heads, or one head and two tails, give a continuous line; while three tails, or one tail and two heads, give a broken line. Starting from the bottom the questor records the appropriate line after each throw, eventually ending up with six lines and the full hexagram. Any lines which are produced by three heads or by three tails are known as *moving lines*, and these are transposed to give a second hexagram, which is taken into account alongside the first. The meaning symbolized by these two hexagrams is then read from the pages of the I Ching, and advice gained as to the relevant courses of future action.

The *I Ching*, or the *Book of Changes*, one of the oldest methods of divination known to mankind, reflects the philosophy of interconnectedness. Dating back to between 1,122 and 770BC, the book has been extensively supplemented by commentaries added by sages thought to include Confucius himself. Briefly, it consists of a set of continuous and broken lines, the former representing "yes" (*yang*) and the latter "no" (*yin*). Each permutation of three lines (*trigram*) or six lines (*hexagram*) is associated with a particular group of meanings. The toss of a series of coins, or the casting of a bunch of yarrow sticks, determines which of these combinations provides the answer to the question.

The I Ching symbolizes the universal presence of opposites: night and day, good and evil, fortune and misfortune, and so on. It recognizes that our perception

I Ching: the Theory

The future develops out of the present. If we accept that all parts of the universe are interconnected, it follows that to know the present is to know the future. However, our knowledge of the present is only partial, and in divination we cannot know which parts of the present relate to which parts of the future. We can only symbolize aspects of the present in the form of numbers. Once these numbers are known, future events can be calculated from them according to a set of fixed laws. In the I Ching, these numbers are revealed by tossing a series of coins, because everything is meaningful in an interconnected universe.

The Trigrams

Anyone who wishes to consult the I Ching fully needs the sixty-four hexagrams and attendant explanations, although working initially with the eight trigrams provides a good introduction to the I Ching. Familiarity with the eight trigrams puts us in the right frame of mind to approach the hexagrams. When working with the trigrams we throw the coins three times only, and ignore moving lines. The eight trigrams, together with their names and meanings, are given here (right).

The symbols are intended to provide suggestive advice, not instructions. Weigh them in the mind, and go cautiously.

Ch'ien: the creative; heaven; the father; active.

K'un: the receptive; earth; mother; passive.

Chen: the arousing; movement; peril; thunder.

K'an: the deep; water; pit; danger.

Ken: the still; high places; arresting progress.

Sun: the gentle; wood; wind; penetration.

Li: the clinging; fire; beauty; brightness.

Tui: the joyous; pleasure; lake; satisfaction.

Glossary

alchemy A medieval forerunner of chemistry concerned with the transmutation of base metals into gold, but also a highly symbolic process of transformation of the spiritual self. The goal of alchemy is to find the philosopher's stone, the agent of both physical and spiritual transformation.

amulet A charm carried about the body to ward off evil.

animus In the Jungian theory of *archetypes*, the male aspect of the female psyche.

anima In the Jungian theory of *archetypes*, the female aspect of the male psyche.

ankh A cross with a loop above the horizontal bar, of particular importance in Egyptian culture as the symbol of life.

archetypes In Jungian theory, universally meaningful symbolic images and ideas that emerge from the collective unconscious. Archetypal images transcend time, culture and heredity, although they may vary in detail between one individual and another.

astrology A system of *divination* based on the interpretation of planetary configurations.

bodhisattva In Buddhism, one who is able to attain the state of *Nirvana*, but delays doing so in order to help others less fortunate.

caduceus A staff, entwined with two serpents and bearing two wings, traditionally carried by the messenger god Hermes. It symbolizes peace and protection.

cardinal points The four chief points of the compass – north, east, south and west.

chakras The psychic and spiritual energy centres in the *etheric body* corresponding to certain organs in the physical body. The chakras symbolize the ascent of man's spiritual development, and form the basis of a system of meditation.

divination Obtaining knowledge of the present and, more specifically, the future by occult means.

etheric body A subtle body, similar in shape to the physical body, through which life-energy flows. The etheric body interpenetrates every atom of the physical body and is visible to clairvoyants as a network of energy streams.

glyph A mark or symbol.

guru A spiritual teacher.

I Ching The Chinese system of *divination* in which the practitioner interprets linear patterns derived by throwing yarrow sticks or coins. The I Ching reflects the philosophy that all events, past, present and future, are interconnected. It is based on 64 hexagrams which represent all basic human situations.

karma In Buddhism and Hinduism, the moral law of cause and effect in which an individual's actions in one life are rewarded or punished in subsequent incarnations.

Kabbalah In the Judaic tradition, a symbolic system of theoretical and practical wisdom providing a means to mental and spiritual growth as well as a symbolic representation of creation. The Kabbalah can be understood through divine revelations in the scriptures. See also *sefiroth*.

macrocosm The "great world", the wider universe. See also *microcosm*.

major arcana The twenty-two picture cards in the Tarot pack, which carry allegorical scenes. The major arcana are often used in *divination* and as a guide in the spiritual journey toward enlightenment.

mandala A symbolic diagram based on geometric shapes and often including a human or divine figure, used as a basis of meditation in Eastern mysticism. It is enclosed in a circle and symbolizes the *macrocosm*, the complementary principles of which are contained in squares or other shapes within the circle.

mantra In Buddhism and Hinduism, a sacred sound symbolizing a particular divine energy, chanted or repeated inwardly during meditation.

microcosm A miniature model of the *macrocosm*. Philosophers saw the human body as a reflection of the universal whole.

minor arcana The four suits (clubs, cups, swords and coins), each of fourteen cards, in the *Tarot* pack.

Nirvana In Buddhist philosophy, the ultimate blessed state to which the practitioner aspires. Nirvana is attained once the Buddhist frees him- or herself from the cycle of continual rebirth by casting aside individual consciousness and its attendant desires.

occult A system of mystical wisdom kept secret by those who practise it.

pentagram (or pentacle) A five-pointed star drawn with five continuous strokes used as a sacred or magical symbol. An upward-pointing pentagram is associated with positive energy, the reverse with negative energy.

sefirah Ten aspects of God, revealed during the creation of the universe and represented in the Kabbalistic *sefiroth*, or tree of life.

sefiroth (or **tree of life**) The most familiar symbol of the *Kabbalah*. The sefiroth graphically sets out the stages of God's manifestation and the relationships that underlie the whole of existence and creation.

shaman A spiritual traveller between our world and the world of the spirits, with whom he (or sometimes she) can commune.

sigil A graphic symbol or magical mark.

stupa In Buddhist tradition, a dome-shaped mound or structure built over the remains of an emperor or spiritual leader.

symbol system A symbolic "map" of reality that represents the fundamental aspects of our emotional and spiritual experience and can be used as a means of exploring and developing the spiritual self.

talisman An object, often a representation of a god or goddess, that is supposed to be invested with the powers of the deity in question.

Tantra An Indian cult in which the practitioner explores the energies (often sexual) of his or her own being and transforms them into subtler, spiritual energies.

Tarot A card pack used for *divination*. See also **major arcana** and **minor arcana**.

yantra A symbolic geometric diagram used as a basis of meditation in Eastern mysticism. It is often constructed from intricately arranged triangles, and typically may be surrounded by lotus leaves, enabling the meditator to contemplate the unity transcending the polarity of opposites. See also *mandala*.

yin yang The two opposing principles of Chinese philosophy determining the destiny of the universe. Yin is feminine, negative and dark; yang is masculine, positive and light.

zodiac A term used in astrology, referring to the band in the sky through which the sun, moon, and planets appear to move, and in which the twelve zodiacal constellations are located.

Further Reading

Binder, P., *Magic Symbols of the World*, London and New York: Hamlyn (1972).

Campbell, J., *The Hero with a Thousand Faces*, Princeton: Princeton University Press, and London: Paladin (1949 and 1988).

Campbell, J., *The Power of Myth*, New York: Doubleday (1988).

Cirlot, J.E., *A Dictionary of Symbols*, New York: Dorset Press (1991).

Cooper, J.C., *An Illustrated Encyclopaedia of Traditional Symbols*, London: Thames and Hudson (1978).

Eliade, M., *From Primitives to Zen*, London: Fount Books (1977).

Filbey, J. and Filbey, P., *The Astrologer's Companion*, Wellingborough, UK: Aquarian Press (1986).

Fischer-Screiber, I. *et al.*, *The Rider Encyclopaedia of Eastern Philosophy and Religion*, London: Rider (1989).

Fontana, D., *Dreamlife: Understanding and Using Your Dreams*, Shaftesbury, UK and Rockport, MA: Element Books (1990).

Fontana, D., *The Meditator's Handbook*, Shaftesbury, UK, and Rockport, MA: Element Books (1992).

Gaskell, G.A., *Dictionary of Symbols and Myth*, New York: Dorset Press (1988).

Hart, G., *A Dictionary of Egyptian Gods and Goddesses*, London and New York: Routledge (1986).

Holroyd, S. and Powell, N., *Mysteries of Magic*, London: Bloomsbury Books (1991).

Huxley, F., *The Way of the Sacred*, London: Bloomsbury Books (1989).

Innes, B., *The Tarot: How to Use and Interpret the Cards*, London: Black Cat (1987).

Jung, C.G. (Ed.), *Man and His Symbols*, London: Aldus Books, and London: Arkana (1964 and 1990).

Jung, C.G., *Analytical Psychology: Its Theory and Practice*, London and New York: Ark Books (1986).

Kokkinou, S., *Greek Mythology*, Athens: Intercarta (1989).

Kurrels, J., *Astrology for the Age of Aquarius*, London: Anaya Publications (1990).

Merrifield, R., *The Archaeology of Ritual and Magic*, London: Batsford (1987).

Morgan, P., *Buddhism*, London: Batsford (1989).

Powell, T.G.E., *The Celts*, London: Thames and Hudson (2nd edn) (1980).

Rawson, P., *Tantra: The Indian Cult of Ecstasy*, London: Thames and Hudson (1984).

Scholem, G., *Kabbalah*, New York: Dorset Press (1987).

Spence, L., *North American Indians: Myths and Legends*, London: Bracken Books (1986).

Thompson, C.J.S., *The Lure and Romance of Alchemy*, New York: Bell Publications (1990).

Van Over, R., *I Ching*, New York: New American Library (1971).

Willis, R. (Ed.), *World Mythology*, New York: Henry Holt, and London: Simon and Schuster (1993).

Picture References

Commissioned illustration by Hannah
Firmin/Sharp Practice

The author and publishers would like to thank the
following museums and photographic libraries for
permission to reproduce their material.

7 Double dragon, after Norton
The Charles Walker Collection, London
9 Francis I guides the Ship of France drawn by the
White Hind, 1515, *Codex Guelf 86.4*
The Ducal Library, Wolfenbuttel/
Weidenfeld & Nicolson Archive, London
10 Jousting figures, detail from Sir Thomas
Holme's book, 1448, Harley 4205 f.37
British Library, London/Weidenfeld & Nicolson
Archive
11 Flaming heart, engraving, George Wither
Private Collection, Lamberhurst, Kent
12 King and Queen in the Fountain of Love,
woodcut from *Rosarium Philosphorum*, 1550
The Charles Walker Collection
14 Hero and damsel
Jan Croot Collection, London
15 Martorelli: *The Beheading of St. John the
Baptist*, c.1450
Museo Diocesano de Barcelona/The Bridgeman
Art Library, London
16 Puvis de Chavannes: *Summer*, mid-19c.
Musée des Beaux Arts, Chartres/Fabbri-Bridgeman
Art Library
17 Zamurrad, Mughal miniature, 1570
Michael Holford Photographs, London
19 Dragon. 19c. embroidered Chinese silk
Private Collection, Hong Kong/The Charles
Walker Collection
20 The Goddess Amaterasu, Japanese woodcut
The Japanese Gallery, London
22 Bison, from the Lascaux Caves, France
Colorphoto Hans Hinz, Allschwill-Basel
23 African mask from the Congo Zombo Tribe
British Museum, London/The Bridgeman Art
Library
24 above Ibis, from the *Book of the Dead of
Neferrenpet*, Thebes, 19th dynasty
Werner Forman Archive, London
24 below Noah's Ark, from *Biblia Sacra
Germanica*, (Nuremberg Bible), 1483
Victoria and Albert Museum, London/The
Bridgeman Art Library
25 Totem pole, Alaska
Hans Schmied, Z.E.F.A.
26 Tezcatlipoca and Quetzalcoatl from *Codex
Borbonicus 3*
Bibliothèque de l'Assemblée Nationale Française,
Paris
27 Vishnu as a fish, from a 17c. Kashmiri text
British Library, London/The Bridgeman Art
Library
29 Ma-Ku creating an orchard from the sea,
painting by Hsiang Kun, 2c. AD
British Library, London/Michael Holford
Photographs
30 Judgement of Ani, detail from an Egyptian
papyrus, c.1,250BC
British Museum, London/Michael Holford
Photographs

31 Emblem of Passion, from the *Playfair Book of
Hours*, French, late 16c.
Victoria and Albert Museum, London/E.T.
Archive, London
32 Golem, from *Anatomica Auri* by J.D. Mylius,
1628
The Charles Walker Collection
33 Krishna and Rhada, Kangra miniature, 1780
Victoria and Albert Museum, London/Michael
Holford Photographs
34 The Symbols of the Alchemical System
revealed, after *Opus Medicochymicum* by J.D.
Mylius, 1618
The Charles Walker Collection
35 Blake: *The Good and Evil Angels*, 1795
The Tate Gallery, London
36 Two Egyptian goddesses and a sacred
crocodile. Fresco in the Villa of the Mysteries,
Pompeii, 1c.AD
Werner Forman Archive
37 Anon: Madonna and Child, with crescent
moon. 13c. Flemish panel
Huis Bergh Collection/The Charles Walker
Collection
38 Point: *The Siren*, 1897
Barry Friedman, New York/The Bridgeman Art
Library
40 Domenico Veneziano: *The Annunciation*
Fitzwilliam Museum, Cambridge
41 The Symbols of the Evangelists, 8c. ms.
Trier Cathedral, Germany/E.T. Archive
42 Utewael: Perseus rescuing Andromeda
Louvre, Paris/Giraudon-Bridgeman Art Library
43 Kali on Shiva, Indian miniature, 18c.
Victoria and Albert Museum, London/E.T.
Archive
45 Bardomandala, Tibet, 19c.
Victoria and Albert Museum, London/E.T.
Archive
47 Magritte: *Le Jouer Secret*, 1927
© ADAGP, Paris and DACS, London 1993
Private Collection/The Bridgeman Art Library
49 Fuseli: *The Nightmare*, 1790-91
Goethemuseum, Frankfurt/Colorphoto Hans Hinz
50 The Eagle and Snake, Tibetan tanka
Private Collection
53 Map of the universe from *The Fine Flower of
Histories* by Logman, 1583
Turkish and Islamic Art Museum, Istanbul/E.T.
Archive
56 The Wheel of Life, Tanka from Eastern Tibet,
c.1930
Robert Bere, Oxford
58 above Leonardo da Vinci: Golden Section
Ancient Art and Architecture Collection, London
58 below Eye, from 18c. Arabic amulet ms.
Dar al Athar al Islammiyyah, Kuwait/The Charles
Walker Collection
60 A Sri Yantra, Nepal, c.1700
John Dugger and David Medalla, London/John
Webb, Surrey
61 Avalokitesvara, Nepalese tanka
Michael Holford Photographs
62 above Dancing ground, or maze, on floor of
Chartres Cathedral, France, 13c.
The Charles Walker Collection
62 below Maze on the ceiling of the Room of the
Labyrinth, Palazzo Ducale, Mantua, Italy, 16c.
Ancient Art and Architecture Collection
64 The Three Wise Men, from *Goelum Stellatum

Christianum* by J. Schiller, 1627
The Charles Walker Collection
65 Astronomical diagram, Kangra, Himachal
Pradesh, 18c.
Ajit Mookerjee, New Delhi/Thames and Hudson,
London
69 The Round Table and the Holy Grail, from
Tristram Book III, f.1
Musée Condé, Chantilly/The Bridgeman Art
Library
71 Arms of Robert Devereux, 3rd Earl of Essex,
died 1646, ms.E16 f.18v
The College of Arms, London
72 Mars in his war chariot, after *Mythologiae,
sine explicationis Fabularum* by Natalis Comites,
1616
The Charles Walker Collection
73 Dürer: *Death, Famine, War and Plague - The
Apocalypse*, 1497/8
Private Collection/The Bridgeman Art Library
74 Orpheus and the Beasts mosaic, Tarsus, 3c.AD
Hatay Museum, Antioch, Turkey/Sonia Halliday
Photographs, Buckinghamshire
75 above Boss from Southwark Cathedral
Ancient Art and Architecture Collection
75 below *The Three Fates*, 19c. engraving
Mary Evans Picture Library, London
76 Knight and dragon, from *Discorides Tractatus
de Herbis*, French, 15c. ms.
Biblioteca Estense, Modena/E.T. Archive
77 Monkey Bridge, print by Hokuju, late 18c.
Victoria and Albert Museum, London/The
Bridgeman Art Library
79 Initial A from *Historia Naturalis* by Pliny the
Elder, Sienese, c.1460
Victoria and Albert Museum, London/E.T.
Archive
80 St. George and the Dragon, Syrian (Melchite)
icon, early period, c.800
Richardson and Kailas Icons, London/The
Bridgeman Art Library
83 above Lord Oliphant, detail from *Seton's
Armorial Crests*
National Library of Scotland, Edinburgh/The
Bridgeman Art Library
83 below Marco Forzata Capodalista from *De
Viris Illustribus*, 15c.
Civic Library, Padua/E.T. Archive
84 above Bewick: Fox, wood engraving, c.1785
Private Collection, London
84 below Canis Major, detail from Southern
Constellation of Argo Navis, from *Atlas Coelestis*
by G. Doppelmayer, 1742
Ann Ronan Picture Library, London
85 Three cats and a rat, English, 13C Harleian
ms.4751 f.30v.
British Library, London
86 Dürer: *Mirror of the Rhetoric* (Icarus and
Daedalus) engraving, 1493
Mary Evans Picture Library
87 Melzi: *Leda and the Swan*, mid-16c.
Galleria degli Uffizi, Florence/The Bridgeman Art
Library
88 Botticelli: *The Birth of Venus*, c.1480
Galleria degli Uffizi, Florence/The Bridgeman Art
Library
89 Octopus, 19c. engraving
Mary Evans Picture Library
90 left Rama, Sita, Lakshman and Hanuman,
detail from Indian painting

Victoria and Albert Museum, London/The
Bridgeman Art Library
90 right Ganesha, from 20c. votive print, Bombay
The Charles Walker Collection
92 above de Vos: *The Rape of Europa*, late 16c.
Museo de Bellas Artes, Bilbao/Index-Bridgeman
Art Library
92 below Bewick: Deer, wood engraving, *c.* 1785
Private Collection
93 Bewick: Sow, wood engraving, *c.* 1785
Private Collection
94 Bewick: Hare, wood engraving, *c.* 1785
Private Collection
96-97 Mermaid of Amboine, 1717
British Library, London/The Bridgeman Art
Library
99 Palmer: *In a Shoreham Garden*
By courtesy of the Board of Trustees of the
Victoria and Albert Museum, London
103 Adam and Eve, Escorial Beatus fol. 18
Real Biblioteca de El Escorial, Madrid/Oronoz,
Madrid
104 Male and female mandrake, 15c. ms.
The Charles Walker Collection
105 Herbal, 12c. ms. Ash 1462 f.17 and 18
The Bodleian Library, Oxford/The Bridgeman Art
Library
106 Bees and beehives, from a bestiary, English
12c. ms.24 f.63
Aberdeen University Library/The Bridgeman Art
Library
107 The Last Supper, 1105/6AD, from the Church
of Our Lady of the Pastures, Asinov
Sonia Halliday Photographs
109 Boat engraving by George Wither
Private Collection, Lamberhurst, Kent
111 Cossier: Prometheus carrying fire, mid-17c.
Prado, Madrid/Index-Bridgeman Art Library
113 Bewick: Neptune, wood engraving
Private Collection, London
114 Volcano, engraving by George Wither
Private Collection, Lamberhurst, Kent
118 left Carved Chinese belt-hook on lapis lazuli
from Badakhstan
The Natural History Museum, London
118 right Agate/**119 top left** Pearls
The Judy Garlick Curio Collection, London
119 top centre Gold coin
Courtesy of Spinks and Son, London
119 top right Jade
Private Collection
119 centre Silver Dollar
Courtesy of Spinks and Son, London
123 The Creation, from *The Luther Bible*
The Bible Society, London/The Bridgeman Art
Library
125 Raising the Maypole, engraved by Alfred
Crowquill for Chambers' Book of Days
Mary Evans Picture Library, London
126 Bewick: Fashionable woman, wood
engraving, *c.* 1790.
Private Collection, London
127 Rubens: *The Judgement of Paris, c.* 1634
Prado, Madrid/The Bridgeman Art Library
128 left Death, English late 15c. ms.
Bodleian Library, Oxford/E.T. Archive
128 right Bewick: *The Grim Reaper*, wood
engraving
Private Collection, London
129 left Detail from *The Creation* by Josephe and

Fouquet, French ms.
Bibliotheque Nationale, Paris/Giraudon-
Bridgeman Art Library
129 above right Lucifer in hell devouring Judas
Iscariot. Woodcut from 1512 edition of *Opere del
divino Danthe*, Venice
The Charles Walker Collection
129 below right Monk, engraving by George
Wither
Private Collection, Lamberhurst, Kent
130 above Christ blessing, from School of
Nonantola, 9c.
Biblioteca Capitolare, Vercelli/E.T. Archive
130 below Christ enthroned, Romanesque Gospel
book, 12c.
Municipal Library, Mantua/E.T. Archive
131 Gold mask. Peru coast, AD400
Tony Morrison South American Pictures
133 François I's entry into Lyon, detail, 1515 ms.
Codex Guelf 86 f.4
Ducal Library, Wolfenbuttel/Weidenfeld &
Nicolson Archive
134 Quetzalcoatl, Artwork based on *Codex
Magliabechiano*
Private Collection, London
135 Saturn, from Solensis Acatus *Phaenomena et
Progostica*, 1569, Cologne
Ann Ronan Picture Library
136 Witch on a broomstick, after Pendle
witchcraft tract, *c.*1621
The Charles Walker Collection
137 van Kessel: The Garden of Eden, 1659
Johnny van Haeften Gallery, London/The
Bridgeman Art Library
138 left Jacob's dream, from 12c. German ms.
Mary Evans Picture Library
138 right Hell, 19c. Japanese painting
Horniman Museum, London/E.T. Archive
139 Patenier: *Charon crossing the Styx,* early 16c.
Prado, Madrid/The Bridgeman Art Library
140 Cellarius: Orbits of the Planets, 1668
By permission of the British Library
(maps C.6.c.2)
141 Astrological Man
Private Collection, London
143 Vishnu Visvarupa, Indian painting, Jaipur,
early 19c.
Victoria and Albert Museum, London/E.T.
Archive
144 Cosmic man, from Agrippa's *De Occulta
Philosophia*, 1532
The Charles Walker Collection
145 above Enochian script, of Dr John Dee. Detail
from Meric Casaubon's *A True and Faithful
Relation ...,* 1657
The Charles Walker Collection
145 below left Symbol of the Secret Order of the
Rosy Cross
Ancient Art and Architecture Collection
145 below right Magical instruments, engraving
from Eliphas Lévi, *Transcendental Magic*, 1896
Private collection, London
146 above Philosopher's stone, from Rosicrucian
Die Hehren der Rosenkreuzer, 1785, Altona
The Charles Walker Collection
146 below Alchemist, detail from the Ripley Scroll
The Charles Walker Collection
147 The Cold Fire, from Michael Maier's *Tripus
Aureus*, 1618
The Charles Walker Collection

148 Philosopher's stone, from *Mutus Liber*, 1677
The Charles Walker Collection
150 Androgyne on lunar demon, 15c. ms
The Charles Walker Collection
151 left The Green Lion, from a 16c. wood
engraving
The Charles Walker Collection
151 centre The Bird of Hermes, detail from the
Ripley Scroll
The Charles Walker Collection
151 right King and Queen in sexual congress.
Woodcut from *Rosarium Philosphorum*, 1550
The Charles Walker Collection
152 Kabbalah, macrocosmic relationship,
woodcut
The Charles Walker Collection
153 Kabbalah, sefiroth, from an Order of the
Golden Cross notebook, *c.*1903
The Charles Walker Collection
154 Illustration by Caroline Church/Garden
Studio
155 Kabbalah, the human body and house, from
Tobias Cohn's *Ma'aseh Tobiyyah*, 1721, Venice
The Charles Walker Collection
156 Zodiacal images, from *Astrorum Scienta*,
1489
The Charles Walker Collection
157 Zodiac, French ms., 15c.
Victoria and Albert Museum, London/E.T.
Archive
158 Mercury from *The Shepheard's Kalendar*,
English, 16c.
Ann Ronan Picture Library
159 Moon and sailors. *De Sphaera* ms., 15c.
Biblioteca Estense, Modena/E.T. Archive
160 Star map, from Sanskrit ms.
British Library, London/E.T. Archive
161 The Goddess Nut surrounded by signs of the
Zodiac. Wooden coffin of Soter, early 2c. AD
British Museum, London/Michael Holford
Photographs
168 Tarot cards, major arcana. Italian, late 19c.
The Charles Walker Collection
169 Tarot cards, two cards from the Waite pack,
late 19c.
The Charles Walker Collection
171 Tarot card, The Fool. French, 18c.
British Museum, London
172-178 Tarot cards. French and Italian 18c. and
19c. packs
British Museum, London
179 Tarot card, The World. Italian, early 19c.
British Museum, London
180 Page from a Tantric palmleaf ms. Khajuraho,
early 19c.
The Charles Walker Collection
181 Tantric iconography, Tibetan painting, 18c.
Gulbenkian Museum, Durham/John Webb
182 The Anahata. Plate 5 from Sir John
Woodroffe's *The Serpent Power*, 1928
The Charles Walker Collection
183 Diagram of the Subtle Body. Kangra,
Himachal Pradesh, *c.*1820
Swen Gahlin, London/John Webb
184 I Ching, the 64 hexagrams in quadrate form,
artwork based on 19c. print
The Charles Walker Collection
185 FuHsi, the first of the Five Legendary
Emperors (to 2,838BC)
The Charles Walker Collection

Index

Page numbers in **bold** type refer to symbols listed in the World of Symbols directory; references to captions in other parts of the book are shown in *italic*.